TROOPER

The Heartwarming Story of the Bobcat Who Became Part of My Family

FORREST BRYANT JOHNSON

Skyhorse Publishing

Praise for *Trooper*

"A charming memoir about a pet bobcat, its owner, family, and friends. Readers who enjoy stories of human-animal friendships, such as Sy Montgomery's *The Good Good Pig* and Irene Pepperberg's *Alex and Me*, will find much to love here."

—*Library Journal*

"The stories [in *Trooper*] are told with compassion, humor, and indeed, some tension as well. This is a read for all ages and of course, will have special significance to anyone who has owned an animal."

—*Las Vegas Review Journal*

"Heartbreaking, warm, beautiful, and emotional, this story didn't just tug on my heart; it stole it. A must-read for any cat, or indeed animal, lover."

—Rachel Wells, author of *A Cat Called Alfie*

"Johnson's accounts of the touching and wondrous tale of Trooper are like having an animal-loving friend explain why we are so in awe of cats—wild and domestic—and other animals. . . That we could all have such animals in our lives to teach, guide, and, in their own way, love us."

—Patricia Barnes-Svarney and Thomas Svarney, authors of *The Handy Biology Answer Book*

"This is a wonderful book, about the amazing relationship that can sometimes form between the wild and humans. Johnson has created something unique and profound, not simply by his telling his story but by truly understanding the differences between wildcats and house pets and the similarities between feral creatures, both human and animal. Trooper knew that Forrest was 'not a very capable cat,' but gave him a chance. Somehow, some way the two formed a miraculous bond, and we, the readers of

this extraordinary work, gain valuable insight into the possibilities between all living things."
—Michael Morse, author of *Mr. Wilson Makes It Home*

"Kind and totally engaging, Forrest's awareness of nature and his love for Trooper make everyday life larger and richer. There are endless adventures and new characters in the form of both people and animals. We learn the history of the desert, about the wildlife, plants, and people, while we spend time with Trooper, Forrest, and his family."
—Clara Weygandt, nature writer

"Johnson's warm and friendly prose keeps the reader involved in the day-to-day interactions between human and animal as well as the exciting encounters that desert life provides. *Trooper* will be of special interest to those who research interspecies communication and to those who esteem and value our animal companions on the planet we share."
—Brad and Sherry Steiger, authors of *Cat Miracles* and *Animal Miracles*

Other Books by Forrest Bryant Johnson

Phantom Warrior
The Last Camel Charge
Hour of Redemption
What Are You Doing Derby Day?
The Strange Case of Big Harry
Basenji—Dog from the Past
Raid on Cabanatuan
Tektite

Skyhorse Publishing books may be purchased in bulk at special discounts for sales promotion, corporate gifts, fund-raising, or educational purposes. Special editions can also be created to specifications. For details, contact the Special Sales Department, Skyhorse Publishing, 307 West 36th Street, 11th Floor, New York, NY 10018 or info@skyhorsepublishing.com.

Skyhorse® and Skyhorse Publishing® are registered trademarks of Skyhorse Publishing, Inc.®, a Delaware corporation.

Visit our website at www.skyhorsepublishing.com.

10 9 8 7 6 5 4 3 2

Library of Congress Cataloging-in-Publication Data is available on file.

Cover design by Tom Lau
Cover photo credit: iStockphoto

Print ISBN: 978-1-5107-5363-1
Ebook ISBN: 978-1-5107-2823-3

Printed in the United States of America.

"You become responsible forever for what you have tamed."

Antoine de Saint-Exupéry, *The Little Prince*

Table of Contents

Prologue

Summer 1987

TO BE TRAPPED INSIDE THE bright yellow blossoms of a cholla
cactus has to be one of the worst ways to die. In the twenty
years that I'd been a guide in the Mojave Desert of southern Nevada,
I'd become keenly aware that animals native to the area possessed
an innate sense of danger when encountering this common shrubby
plant. And so, on this hot July morning, as I was exploring the
Mojave for yet another scenic spot for the next day's tourists, I was
astonished to hear a rather odd sound coming from devil cholla, the
low-growing cactus near me.

I had been walking above a wide ravine that cut deep into the
desert floor by generations of fast-moving water, although it was
totally dry at this time. There had been no rain in neighboring Las
Vegas or across the Spring Mountains for over seventy days. I had
just paused by the ravine's edge to enjoy the wilderness's beauty,
watching the distant peaks and the vast treeless terrain sprinkled

with wild sage, yucca, creosote bushes, and variety of cacti. The world seemed utterly tranquil, promising a perfect day ahead.

But suddenly I heard a baby's cry. At least it sounded like the muffled sob of a newborn. The nearest home was almost a mile away, so obviously nothing had come from there. And then who would be so cruel as to abandon an infant in the Mojave's unbearable heat? Had someone placed a baby in the ravine during the night? A sick feeling rippled through me. But then the sound came again, albeit a little different this time.

Could it be the cry of an injured animal, perhaps a ferocious coyote or cougar? There is always danger when encountering a wounded beast, especially cougars known to attack humans. That's why I always carry a loaded pistol when exploring the Mojave—although I am aware that such a small weapon is not likely to provide much protection from a charging mountain lion.

Still, having a gun and being an excellent shot allowed me to investigate the source of these peculiar cries. I could not walk away after the haunting thought that they might have come from a human infant. And so, disregarding possible danger, I slid down the embankment while pulling my pistol from its holster. Then I paused, waiting for another sound to determine which way I should move.

There was no breeze in the ravine, with the morning heat having reached a near-suffocating intensity between high walls. Then another cry. I began walking slowly in its direction as my eyes searched the sandy floor for tracks or disturbed earth. I moved cautiously, my footsteps making no sound in the soft path. Determination and curiosity smothered rationality and logic. Sweat began to bead on my forehead, running in little streams down my cheeks to offer some cooling.

Then I saw movement at the base of a yellow-green cholla. Something was there. I held my breath as I raised the pistol high. Then quickly I realized there was no danger, so I un-cocked the weapon, returning the pistol to its holster.

A small brown animal was trapped in the cholla, crying as it struggled to escape. Its fur was a mangled mess, dried blood and puncture wounds visible at its shoulder. A far larger beast, most likely a coyote, seemed to have decided to have the tiny critter for dinner. As I moved closer, I figured the thing to be either a small domestic cat or a large household kitten, most likely lost in the wilderness. I wondered how the animal reached this distant spot so far from its home. Who did it belong to, and how had it managed to survive such dreadful wounds? And how did it escape its attacker?

The poor creature apparently avoided death by hiding in the cholla, but now it was trapped in its once safe haven. I had a tough decision to make. If I abandoned the little cat, it would surely face a slow, horrible death in the ravine. Should I end its suffering with a bullet? I could not do that. But if I carried it back to my home, I'd never find its rightful owner.

The cat moved again slightly, making pitiful sounds. I knew what I had to do. Kneeling next to the small bundle, I slowly freed it from the cholla's clutches. Then I removed my T-shirt and, lifting the cat carefully, wrapped the white cloth around it.

By now a quick check had determined that I was holding a male kitten. Cradling my small charge next to my chest, I called my wife from my cell, asking her to alert the Sun Animal Hospital that I was bringing in a badly injured cat. The cat had managed to push his head slightly from the T-shirt to gaze up at me. And as one leg protruded from the T-shirt, I noticed that his paw appeared large for his body size. It made no impression at the time, focusing as I was on getting this poor baby to the vet.

Speaking softly, I muttered reassuring words to the small creature. These made me feel better, and I hoped the gentle murmur of my voice created much-needed reassurance for him. Walking swiftly back to my car, I thought I heard the kitten begin to purr, softly and very low at first, then increasing the volume. I looked down to see huge dark eyes staring at me. It was my first experience with a cat, and it felt both quite strange and sort of wonderful. In a minute I had reached the car, placing a now apparently sleeping kitten next to me. In less than fifteen minutes we arrived at the veterinary hospital.

CHAPTER 1

My New Friend

"I simply can't resist a cat, particularly a purring one."

Mark Twain

ONCE UP ON A TIME, NOT long ago, I had a most unusual friend. We met in the Mojave Desert near the glittering city of Las Vegas, when he was very young, and I not so young. And we remained close companions for nineteen years. And as all friends need to do, we learned many things from one another.

This friend was a cat. He was not an ordinary feline, but a kitty from the wild—a bobcat, as such creatures are called in many parts of the US; they are wild animals, even when captured very young, are not easily domesticated and seldom make good pets. Keeping a wild critter is illegal in some states; others have strict restrictions or require specific permits for their live possessions.

One question bothered me about my buddy. Is it fair to tame and keep a bobcat as a pet? Or should it be released, returned to the wild once it is strong enough to survive on its own? I had seriously

1

considered all options before deciding to raise this particular feline as a member of my family, to live in my home, which, as it happened, is located at the edge of the Mojave Desert. Our family bobcat (as he became) would always be given freedom to come and go as he pleased. And then decide whether to return to the wild or remain with us.

My considerations also included knowing that genetically the bobcat is closely related to domestic felines. Could our cat eventually behave like a house pet if offered the same environment? Bobcats are loners once they leave their mother's care. Unlike African lions, for example—such as Elsa, forever immortalized in the film *Born Free*—a bobcat does not belong to a pride, nor does it need any group to help learn survival skills. And then my cat had lost his own mother before he reached the age of two months. Could he remain alive in a desert that provided such limited food and water?

The deciding factor came from alarming statistics supplied by the Nevada Department of Wildlife Conservation. Over 10,200 bobcats had been trapped or killed in the year before I found my kitten. There were mostly shot by hunters or poachers lacking permits and functioning out of hunting season. Beginning in the 1990s, a growing middle class in China and Russia had created the demand for luxury furs, the then favorite being the bobcat's shiny and beautiful pelt.

And so I decided that returning this cat to the wild was tantamount to a death sentence. But how would anyone domesticate a wild creature? Would it be an impossible task undertaken in the effort to save him? I understood that each situation and each animal is different. Like humans, cats possess their own personalities and function at different intelligence levels. To my delighted surprise, I discovered in only a few weeks that my cat possessed a superior brain. This I concluded by judging his response to various situations and his ability to learn and react to verbal instructions.

One of the greatest questions of mankind has been, can animals and humans communicate? In 1978 there was a celebrated experiment with Koko, the gorilla, and his person where each seemed to "know" what the other wanted. The ancient Greeks had a special form of communication they called "telepathy," when a perception or feeling was believed to be transmitted by thought or feeling. And the Japanese relied on an expression called *e-shin, den-shin*, or messages sent from one mind to another through shared feelings. Did I "talk" to my cat? Not exactly . . .

Ask anyone who has ever been owned by a cat and you'll learn that these remarkable animals seem to sense when a person is anxious or depressed or even ill. And then proceed to help as best as a cat can, with warmth and love, cuddling and closeness.

My special friend and I shared much during our time together. That's what I write about here. Soon after we met, I decided to call him Trooper. It is an army name I picked up during my years in the military. It refers to a soldier (or anyone) with an especially tough fighting spirit who overcomes difficulties despite all odds. Just as Trooper did, and taught me to do.

CHAPTER TWO

"Will He Live?"

"In the desert the line between life and death is sharp and quick."

Frank Herbert, *Dune*

I HAD NEVER OWNED A cat before Trooper. And so, I had imagined felines to be fuzzy little things that hunted birds and mice, preferring to prowl the neighborhood at night. But I always hated to see any animal suffer, certainly including a cat.

"I don't know if you'll live or die," I told my unresponsive bundle as we hustled through the doors of the animal hospital. "But you deserve a chance, and I'm going to see that you get it." And then we both proceeded to the receptionist.

"I have a wounded cat," I told her. "Found him in the desert in a cholla patch."

"Yes, Mr. Johnson," she said, leading the way into an examination room. "Your wife called. Doctor Marg will be in to see you in a moment. She's our resident cat expert." The girl tossed a wide grin at us. "And she can make the meanest cat calm down, using only her voice."

4

And so I was left alone with the little cat with the big feet. Doctor Marg entered the room within minutes, turning out to be a large woman well beyond the age of fifty. But when she spoke, her voice was soft, very different from her masculine appearance.

"Put the little fellow down on the table so we can look at the damage," she said. And then, with a single gentle motion, removed my T-shirt from the cat.

"Well, now," she exclaimed. "What do we have here? How interesting!"

"He's a neighbor's cat," I said. "Maybe caught by a coyote. There aren't any big dogs in our area to cause this kind of damage."

The doctor was quiet as she examined our patient. "I'm giving him a shot as a relaxant so we can go to work. You're lucky he didn't regain consciousness and claw you to ribbons. This kitty doesn't belong to one of your neighbors. He's not a house cat."

"So where did he come from?"

"From the desert, Mr. Johnson; where you found him. This is a bobcat kitten, not a fully-grown domestic cat. See? His spots are beginning to fade. I'm guessing he's about six weeks old."

"A bobcat! But his ears are not pointed and . . . and, well, his tail seems too long."

"He may look like a full-grown cat, but he is only a youngster," Dr. Marg said. "Like people, not all cats are created the same. Some have big ears, others small. Still, they are people—same with bobcats. Some have pointed ears, some have tufts of fur at the top. This particular one has slightly rounded ears. As for the tail, feel here." She guided my hand to the cat's tiny backside.

"Feel the bones," she said. "His tail should have ended here, at the last bone, and should be much shorter."

"But can you save him?"

"Oh, certainly. First we need to get X-rays to check for fractures and look for internal damage." She wrapped the little cat in a fresh white cloth, scooping him up in her arms. Then turned to me. "You understand that this is a wild creature. He has never known human attention or love . . ."

"But," I interrupted, "he was purring while I carried him from the desert."

"Even mountain lions purr. Cats purr under stress or if they are content and comfortable." Then she added, like an afterthought, "He may be a hybrid."

"A what?"

"Hybrid. Once in a while a wild cat will mate with a domestic one. It's rare, but it does happen. I must tell you, as well, that this work may get expensive."

I didn't hesitate for a second. "I want you to do everything to save him."

"You may wait in my office if you like. I'll be back shortly to review everything."

She returned in less than fifteen minutes, with a clipboard tucked under her arm. "He'll pull through just fine," she said. "He's a tough kitty—comes from felines who survive in this desert against difficult odds. The x-rays show no broken bones. No damage to organs that we can tell. We cleaned the puncture wounds . . . should heal in a week. We're injecting fluids and other medicines into him now. In two or three days he'll be strong enough for vaccines."

She paused, staring at me for a reaction. I swallowed to control my nerves.

"Doctor . . ." I hesitated to ask the question, fearing rejection. "May I keep him?"

She was clearly curious about a motive. "You need to know some things before making that decision." And then she listed them: the law in Nevada that governed wild animals; the enormous patience needed to train them; the fact that they may return to the wild, regardless of human love and care.

And then she explained, "You realize that he won't remain a cute little kitty forever. He'll gain maybe twenty or thirty pounds. His claws will also grow, and he'll need lots of things to scratch on. A cat post will help, but he could soon start on your furniture."

"I understand," I said, although the details were becoming a little worrisome.

But still I said, "I saved him. I'm going to pay to patch him up, make sure that he'll have plenty of freedom to come or go."

"Do you have other . . . pets?" Dr. Marg asked.

"No. And I was never a cat person. But this fellow is different. I would like to stay in touch with you and your staff, keep you posted on our progress."

"Of course, and thank you. For us and medically speaking, this will be an opportunity to study a wild cat while he is in our care. For you, there is a list of what you need for the new arrival: First, find a strong crate to transport him, one that can hold, say, thirty pounds; never use cardboard since he'll claw that to pieces in seconds."

"OK," I said, nodding. "But by the way, do you have any idea as to how he escaped and ended up in a cactus patch?"

"Most likely a pack of coyotes attacked his family. A grown bobcat can whip a single coyote with ease. But those brutes usually attack in pairs or as a pack. Coyotes possess an excellent hunting system. One or two will distract the largest victim, then the others attack from the sides. It seems that our little cat was shaken by a single coyote, who was trying to kill him that way. But then the attacker lost his bite—his grip. So the cat went flying into the cholla. No doubt the coyote waited for his prey to emerge, then finally gave up. No way would a coyote willingly enter a cholla patch. You know how dangerous those needles can be and so do coyotes."

"I sure do. You can pull the needles out, but the sheaves will remain and cause a great deal of pain."

Then we set the next day for another visit and agreed that he should be neutered during the several days he remained in her care.

Leaving the vet, I knew that a great adventure awaited me. Raising a bobcat would be no normal feat. But driving home, I also realized something else; something much more pressing. How would I tell my wife that I had just adopted a baby bobcat?

CHAPTER 3

The Adventure Begins

"You will always be lucky if you know how to make friends with a strange cat."

Early American proverb

"**H**OW BIG WILL HE GET?" my wife, Chiaki, inquired with serious concern.

"A little larger than a house cat," I replied.

"How much is *a little*?" she asked me knowingly.

"Maybe twice as much," I confessed. "But," I added, "I don't think he'll get that big."

"Oh," she said with no emotion.

My wife, who was born in Japan, was unfamiliar with bobcats. She thought it strange that a wild animal would be named "Bob."

I had to explain that "bob" referred to the species' normally truncated tail. Trooper's tail, I noted, was longer than a typical bobcat's, but not as long as one belonging to a house cat.

After a moment of silence she asked, "Suppose he bites someone?"

"Bobcats don't attack people, not even in the wild. They are very shy. Like any cat, he may hunt rats, mice, birds, and rabbits. But if we feed him hearty cat food, maybe he won't need to hunt."

"I can fix him some chicken now and then," she suggested with lukewarm enthusiasm, "and I'll share the fish that I eat."

"I'm sure he'll like that," I replied. "He's really very cute. Big ears, big feet, and fuzzy face. The doctor had to clip his fur to treat the wounds, but it will get thick again just before winter. He purrs and is playful like any other kitten. Of course, he's very curious."

My wife and I had entirely different upbringings. I was born in Louisville to middle class parents. My mother was from Atlanta and was a university graduate. My father, a high school graduate, grew up in a small town in southern Kentucky.

My early memories center on my strong desire to explore the wooded wilderness of Kentucky, especially its mysterious limestone caves and the animals that inhabit its remote places. This drive to explore was, in part, the result of my parents introducing me to exciting adventure stories: *The Last of the Mohicans, King Solomon's Mines,* and *Seven Pillars of Wisdom.*

It was my father who first led me into the dark wilderness. A fanatic on Kentucky history, he instructed me in the art of survival, techniques employed by early explores like Daniel Boone and George Rogers Clark. My father once said, "When you are age twelve you must know how to shoot a rifle straight and throw a tomahawk." He was serious. I qualified but fortunately never found it necessary to use the tomahawk for anything but chopping wood.

When I reached college age, I had to put aside exploring and concentrate on learning how to survive in a business world. I graduated from the University of Louisville, paying tuition by working at the YMCA in the evenings and lifeguarding at a local country club during the summers. I had dreamed of going on to medical school, but had neither the necessary funds nor grades required for admission. So after graduation I went to work in the laboratory of a local industrial coatings manufacturer. Both the company and I soon learned that I was a poor chemist; my career was going nowhere fast. Then the US Army stepped in and changed my life for the next few years. I began to experience a quantity of wilderness life. The army has always been able to uncover remote places to practice. I started with the rank of private, commissioned a lieutenant a year later, and finished with the rank of captain. I returned to my old industrial company, only this time in the field of sales, which was a much better fit for me.

I was assigned the Iowa sales territory, and later transferred to Chicago where I survived long, very cold winters. But my marriage did not do well as the executive life of travel and entertainment required me to spend much time away from my three children. The balance between family and job was one I did not maintain well at all. Divorce ultimately separated us. My ex-wife and children moved to Phoenix and I, too, longed to relocate to a desert, any desert, just so long as it was warmer than Chicago. But I had to remain in the north for a few more years as that executive income was required to support both myself and my separated family until the children became adults. The army had trained me in desert survival and I developed a love for such an environment. So, one day I decided to become an "executive drop out," turned in the company car, and gave up a nice salary and expense account living and drove an old truck to Las Vegas. Las Vegas was then a small town of only 150,000 people at the time (now it is over 2.6 million) and sits in the middle of the Mojave Desert. Gambling, shows, night club life—nothing would distract me from my new goal, creating a desert scenic tour business. While discussing my ideas with members of an established tour company, I was introduced to a single (also divorced) lady my age. Thus, my relationship with Chiaki Keiko began.

Her given name was Chieko but I called her by her stage name, Chiaki, and often a nickname I gave her, "Chi." She had, like the cat we would soon own, had earned the title "trooper." She survived a number of changes in her life, each time emerging a little stronger for the experience.

Chiaki grew up in the city of Sapporo, Japan, during the last days of World War II, survived the Allied bombings, and later attended a Catholic high school run by German nuns who spoke English and Japanese, as well as German. In those days, Japanese civilians had very little to eat, as the Imperial army had taken most everything from the people, including food, for the war effort. At the end of the war, her first encounter with Americans occurred when several soldiers entered her family's home, apparently searching for someone. She and her siblings were terrified. During the war, the Imperial army had announced by radio that American soldiers rape and murder all women and eat children. Yet, she discovered that the GIs were professional, friendly, and harmless. She remembered one odd thing: the barbarians, as the Americans were called, did not remove their shoes when they entered the home.

Perhaps Americans were barbarians but she soon learned that they had created beautiful music like swing, ballads, and jazz. Chiaki began to sing some of the American songs even though, at the time, she did not understand the meaning of each word. The nuns at her school discovered that Chiaki had a beautiful singing voice and encouraged her to enter a contest sponsored by a local radio station. She won handily, singing Nat King Cole's classic ballad, "Too Young." This earned her a trip to Tokyo, where she won more contests by singing American classics in the original English. This was an unusual accomplishment at the time. Very few Japanese singers could sing in English with any quality. Soon Chiaki became one of Japan's top recording artists of the 1960s.

A few executives from Tokyo radio station JOQR had an idea for a new kind of late-night talk show. Those tuned in to JOQR one night were shocked to hear the mellow voice of a woman discussing her feelings about life, adventure, love, and men. For the first time in Japan a woman was discussing those subjects over the radio as she played recorded songs. The show was an overnight success with the already popular Chiaki Keiko as DJ. This gig led to her discovery by American talent scouts who brought her to Las Vegas, where she was booked at several different casino-hotels. She married and Las Vegas became her home. Unfortunately, the marriage failed and Chiaki retired from performing professionally.

Back in the early '80s, Japanese tourists were swarming into Las Vegas. Most were serviced by Japanese tour companies that had branch offices in Las Vegas. And that is where I found Chiaki, working as a tour guide and interpreter. As our relationship developed I suggested that we start a tour business, but she wisely believed that such a venture would not be successful unless we had a truly unique idea to attract business. As a guide she had accumulated a vast knowledge of what gifts the Japanese craved. These included designer items, leather belts, handbags, and wallets. But they were also buying unusual items to take back home to loved ones.

With limited funds, we started a small gift shop that sold beef jerky (customers usually bought a dozen bags each) and designer items we purchased at discount stores, marking the prices back to "retail." Our volume of purchase was so great that representatives of the manufacturers of some of those items tracked us down, issued credit, and sold us new items at a wholesale price. Our profit soared and we were ready to move our shop into a major Strip hotel. The hours were long, but we were doing something we love to do—work with people. We often remained at the shop until it closed at 2 a.m.

From the moment we met, I had a plan to slowly introduce Chiaki to the strange but beautiful Mojave Desert. I fed her little spoonfuls of information on the plants and animals and led her into it so she could see, smell, and experience its rugged beauty. She eventually fell in love with it as I had.

At first I thought she might be acting the part of good Japanese wife by pacifying me with pseudo-enthusiasm. But I discovered she truly enjoyed the freedom, peace, and quiet—not to mention the fresh air—of our desert home.

Together, we read everything we could find about the Mojave Desert, which would eventually become a valuable asset for our business venture as tour guides. The Mojave, we learned, is one of the three Great Deserts, as they are called, in the United States, covering the entire southern part of Nevada and California, and extending into northern Mexico. Its birth began about 250 million years ago, when what is now southern Nevada emerged from a shallow sea. Sand dunes, the result of violent winds, formed 180 million years ago and were fossilized into sandstone. This sandstone often took shape as spectacular rock formations. Dynamic changes followed as the earth's crust folded, faulted, and fell, often aided by volcanic activity. Finally, about 15,000 years ago, the earth settled down to become the desert landscape we see today. The Mojave is known as a "high desert" as most of it is 2,000 feet above sea level. The only exception is the Death Valley area, which is at and below sea level in some places.

The first Europeans to enter the Mojave Desert were the Spaniards. In 1604 Don Juan de Onate y Salazar led a gold prospecting expedition up the Colorado River and encountered a nation of tall, powerfully built Native Americans who called themselves the *macave* ("the people who live by the river"), from which the word "Mojave" is derived.

Some are surprised to learn that there are a variety of wildlife who call the Mojave Desert home. Surviving in this harsh environment requires a special strategy for finding water and avoiding the worst of the heat. Owls and bats are active only at night when temperatures are lower. Creatures such as lizards, snakes, rodents, and insects are active during the early morning hours and at dusk, seeking shelter in cool burrows during the heat of the day.

Some animals have evolved physiologically to enable them to regulate body heat. Jackrabbits, for example, have large ears lined with small blood vessels, allowing air to cool their blood as it circulates. At higher elevations, mule deer and bighorn sheep will drink enough water at limited resources to last them several days. Predators such as the coyote, little kit fox, gray fox, bobcat, mountain lion (aka cougar and puma), and desert badger drink water when available, but are not dependent on it as the moisture from the prey they eat, such as small rodents and birds, satisfies their needs. All of these animals rest most of the day, hunting at dusk and dawn.

Birds, which are known carnivores, such as the red-tailed hawk, golden eagle, and roadrunner, hunt during the day. The raven is believed to be the most successful omnivore in the desert sky.

The feral horses, commonly referred to as mustangs, and donkeys, called burros, originally introduced to the area by early Spanish conquistadores, have been relocated further north where there is more natural food and water. However, a few can still be seen roaming the Mojave.

The gentle reptile known as the desert tortoise spends most of his life in underground burrows to escape from the harsh summer and winter weather of the desert. This government-protected tortoise is the largest reptile in the Mojave Desert and is a vegetarian with a special taste for flowers.

Through our research, during that first year of our marriage Chi and I learned the names of most of the desert plants, identifying which were safe to eat and which ones weren't. My small library of books on desert survival provided the basic knowledge we needed. I had no plans for us to actually put all that information to the test. It was simply good to know and gave us a greater connection to the desert. Now I would need her help in raising a kitten from the wild who had not yet learned how to hunt or find water.

"Well, we had better get him some toys," my wife said, "and a cat tree to climb on."

My sales pitch was working. Or perhaps it was simply that I had a very loving and understanding wife, who, like myself, possessed an element of curiosity about all natural things.

We had no pets and our children were now grown. It was only the two of us. So, deciding to raise Trooper as a kind of surrogate child, we embarked on a shopping spree for, among other things, a cat door (which I'd have to enlarge after two months); a six-foot cat tree; a litter box (which he never used, preferring the great outdoors); and a travel crate made of steel, guaranteed to hold a forty-pound animal.

I encouraged my wife to think of Trooper as an ordinary cat, and to tell anyone who inquired that he was a stray. A very large stray.

Fortunately, my work schedule permitted me to spend time with Trooper each day. He seemed to recognize me the moment I entered the room and purred when I scratched the top of his head through his cage.

Finally the day came for me to take him home. Of course, I was nervous. Despite all my research on bobcats, cats in general, and numerous conversations with the hospital staff regarding Trooper's behavior, I remained uncertain as to what to expect once he arrived home.

Before the cat could be released, I had a consultation with Doctor Marg.

"I must tell you, Mr. Johnson, your Trooper is a real favorite with my staff," Doctor Marg told me. "To our surprise, he is very affectionate and enjoys being stroked. We can pick him up to move him about, but he does not like being held for more than a few seconds. That is not unusual. Wild animals, when young, may like our attention, but our affection is strange for them, and being lifted off the ground makes them feel insecure."

"Does he growl when you do that?" I asked.

"A little. But mostly he kicks his back legs. Keep that in mind. Those claws are dangerous.

"It may sound strange, but I am a bit envious," she said with a grin. "You are in for an interesting education. I wish I could be the one to raise Trooper, but I have my work here. But I plan to follow your progress with Trooper."

"Yes," I replied. "My wife and I have discussed our . . . experiment. We've decided we'll meet the cat halfway. We'll try to domesticate him but with very few restrictions, meaning he'll essentially have the run of the house."

Doctor Marg chuckled. "That will be interesting. According to my nurse, Trooper knows when you enter the door. He hears your voice before she does and presses his face against the cage with ears forward."

"Maybe he knows who saved him," I said.

"Oh, yes. You'll learn that cats are superior observers. They will know the sound of your footsteps, the sound of your car engine, and learn your time clock—when you wake and when you sleep. Instinctively he would be a dawn and dusk hunter, but he'll be pulled by curiosity to conform to your schedule."

"I'm concerned about how high-strung he'll be," I confessed. "I've read that most wild animals exhibit nervous behavior."

"It's much too early to know. Like all kittens, he'll be curious about everything. That is how they learn. Their little brain records it all. At a certain age, kittens learn faster than humans. We believe their early intelligence may equal to that of a three- or four-year-old human. They can't ask questions, so they must learn by experiment. Like any child, he'll need lots of sleep. He'll even learn your moods. If you are sad, you won't be able to hide it from your cat."

"Really?" I blinked at her.

"Yes, and unlike we humans, cats don't hold a grudge. They are the most forgiving creatures on earth."

"Well, I hope I won't have to ask for his forgiveness," I said.

"While you are recording your observations, Mr. Johnson, we'll want to know more about his vision. We don't know if the medication has had any adverse effect on that. Most cats, so you know, have a 285-degree field of vision. Trooper may have even more. This could be difficult for you to judge.

"I'll stay alert for anything unusual."

"The same with sound," she continued. "Cats hear sounds at much higher frequencies than we do, about five times higher." She paused to read notes on her clipboard. "He has had all his shots and the necessary blood tests. They'll have your paperwork and rabies tag at the reception desk. I hope you have no objection, but we placed a locator computer chip under his skin so you can be notified if he's lost and found."

"Glad you did."

"One more thing. Trooper gave us all a surprise yesterday evening as we were closing the clinic."

"Yes?"

"Well, you already know he purrs. He will make any number of sounds, and some of them might be quite terrifying. As we were closing the clinic last night we heard a loud scream. We rushed back to find Trooper sitting peacefully next to his food bowl. A bobcat scream can be ten times louder than an ordinary house cat's, and their growl is even more ferocious. They often combine this with a variety of hissing. Just as young hound dogs bay or howl to hear themselves, Trooper discovered he could scream and decided to practice for really no reason. You might want to educate your neighbors and tell them not to be alarmed."

"I'll prepare them," I said. "We plan to move to a place with more land in less than a year. It's a small ranch with lots of trees and space."

"Excellent. But remember, if he gets to be too much of a problem, bring him to me and we will reintroduce him to the wild. He'll be strong enough to survive in a year's time. But if we wait too long, his natural hunting skills will fade and that could be dangerous for him."

As I signed the release forms in the reception area, a young nurse entered the room carrying my travel crate. "We're going to miss this fellow," she said, beaming.

"I'll bring him back for visits."

Trooper was quiet until I started the car, at which point he released a variety of snarls and shook his crate violently. My voice had no calming effect on him. However, the moment we pulled into the driveway of our home and I turned the engine off, he became peaceful again.

Chi sat on the couch, her hands clasped in front of her as she calmly waited. She didn't appear excited about the coming event. But a number of concerns raced through my mind.

Would the cat leap out and attack us? Even though he was only an eight-pound kitten, his claws worried me. *Would he race through the sliding glass doors, which Chi had opened?* I knew at least that he could not escape our small backyard, for it was completely enclosed by a block wall which was much too high for a young cat to scale.

I slid the latches of the crate back slowly, held my breath, and gently opened the top. For a few moments Trooper sat motionless and stared at me. Then he raised his head out of the crate to conduct a visual survey of the strange world around him. His eyes fell on a bowl of dry cat food Chi had placed on the kitchen floor. His nose twitched and he gracefully sprang from the crate and rushed to the kitchen. A crunching sound told us he accepted it.

His eyes then caught something in the backyard and he rushed out the open door, crossed the little wooden bridge spanning a narrow fish pond, and quickly crawled into a grove of bamboo in the corner of the yard. He remained hidden somewhere in that cluster of greenery for more than two hours while Chi and I discussed what to do next. We decided it was best to simply wait and see if Trooper would return for dinner. But I could not yet think of food. My stomach felt twisted as I sat and stared out into the yard, trying to control my worry for our mysterious pet.

CHAPTER 4

How to Domesticate a Wild Kitten

"An ordinary kitten will ask more questions than any five-year-old."

Earl Van Vechten

HOW DOES ONE BEGIN TO domesticate a baby wild cat? In my saga of the relationship between man and feline, it became my most interesting challenge.

First, I considered the environment my little friend once thought of as home, and what he might have learned before we met. His mother would have provided everything for him, from food to a warm and comfortable den for shelter. Bobcats, like all cats, are trained by their mothers in the art of stalking and hunting, as it is a path to their future survival. True, this is an instinct the cats are born with, but it is perfected for practical use by the mother.

After much thought, I concluded that Trooper's mother was apparently killed by coyotes before he had the opportunity to learn much of anything. If she had survived the coyote attack, then she would have returned to search for her young. But the day I found Trooper I saw no evidence of that, no cat tracks in the dirt, which

19

would indicate she had not been in the area. I did see coyote prints, easily identifiable by the extended claw marks. A bobcat would leave no such print, as their claws are retracted when they walk. Sleeping and playing had probably occupied most of his time. I thought this relative lack of education might work to my advantage. He had had little experience living "wild." I guessed that his family had been training or hunting when they were ambushed by a pack of coyotes. No doubt his mother had put up a fight to give her kittens time to escape to the safety of their den. The evidence suggested that only Trooper, by a twist of fate, had survived.

So, at first, my job seemed simple. All I'd have to do is provide him with food, a safe, warm place to sleep, and supervision during play. (Play is essential to the development of most animals and it usually involves siblings.) Though Trooper invented many of his own games, which he alone enjoyed, when he and I played together, things often got a little rough. (I still have small scars on my arms, which were unintentionally caused by his sharp claws and teeth.)

Chi and I planned to impose some restrictions on Trooper when he was in the house, but could not agree on what these should be. Clawing on wooden furniture would surely be forbidden and climbing drapes a big no-no, as well. We knew what to expect from a spoiled child, but had no idea how a spoiled cat, especially a wild one, would behave.

That first day with Trooper at home, I was reading at the kitchen table, still trying to calm my nerves, while my wife cooked dinner. A quick glance towards the small bamboo grove outside our sliding glass doors confirmed that Trooper had us under observation. The bamboo stalks moved from time to time, revealing the cat's fuzzy face peering out.

Finally he broke from the bamboo and moved slowly to the pond. The goldfish swimming about captured his attention. How strange a picture it must have been for him. He had never seen fish before, nor a pool of water. There had been no rain in our part of the desert for months. As a kitten, the moisture he needed came from his mother's milk and whatever he ate.

Trooper crouched low as he studied the fish. He reached out his paw and cautiously touched the surface. He withdrew the paw quickly, studied the drops of water on his fur, and then licked it dry. He repeated the experiment and the fish responded by darting about and breaking the surface with a splash.

What a wonderful discovery for the cat! He had found a large source of water and interesting creatures in it to play with. Then he decided to take a long drink of the pond water. What is it about cats that impels them to drink dirty water when fresh, clean stuff is available?

"Maybe he thinks if he drinks all the water he can get closer to the fish," I commented to Chi, upon observing this odd behavior. I couldn't think of any other explanation.

I watched Trooper stroll across our little wooden bridge and enter the kitchen through the sliding doors. He paused for a quick scratch from me before heading to his bowl for a snack. The next object for investigation was the carpet covered cat tree, which he gave a good clawing before bounding to the top platform, looking around, and leaping to the kitchen table, landing directly in front of me. That gave Chi and me a jolt as we had no idea what to expect from a wild kitten. But for an animal near death just a few weeks earlier, he displayed surprising acrobatic abilities.

What happened started a series of events which gave us lasting memories for years to come.

Chi had a yellow teddy bear that I had given to her when we first met. It stood at about nine inches tall. She placed the toy against one table leg near the cat's food bowl to watch his reaction. Of course, Trooper noticed the bear the moment he hit the floor and sniffed it carefully.

"Yellow Bear is for you, Trooper," Chi said.

The cat looked up at her. Then he seized the bear in his mouth and carried it to his food bowl. We watched as he placed the bear face-down in the kibble, where it remained for a full two minutes while the cat studied it with apparent concern. After that, he carried it to the water bowl, where it received a quick dunking. Then he returned the bear, dripping wet, to its original position against the table leg. We thought that maybe he remembered the time when his mother first attempted to wean him and his siblings by introducing solid food. Perhaps she returned to their den with a freshly killed rabbit or some small creature. She would have carried her kittens, one at a time, to the dinner and waited as each sampled that new kind of food.

It appeared as if Trooper was sharing his most treasured possession—food—with a toy. After a few days of feeding, Trooper apparently concluded that Yellow Bear had had enough to eat. It then became his sleeping companion. We soon learned that the bowl of dry food would be offered to any object he cared for or considered important.

A week later we decided to begin the cat's education in earnest by introducing him to certain key words: Yellow Bear, dry food, yum-yum (for all other food), water, "Mama" for Chi, and "Johnson" for me. This proved a good test of Trooper's ability to recognize by association things in his daily life. In time, his understanding would exceed our expectations. Chi could say to the cat, "Go find Johnson," and Trooper would explore the house until he found me. At first, he'd made a sharp barking sound, like a small dog, while he searched for me. I had no idea that cats made such noises until I heard it from my kitty's mouth. But from later watching a old Disney wildlife TV show, I learned that mother wild cats, including mountain lions, use a similar bark to call their young. Trooper remembered the bark and used it to locate me, no doubt expecting me to answer in a similar fashion. As months went by we heard the bark less and less, and eventually not at all. He had learned to depend on his keen sense of smell and hearing to find me. Cats can hear much higher-pitched sounds than humans, going as high as even an octave above that of a dog. Further, cat ears can swivel from forward to side to the rear, and their ability to see in very dim light with a vast visual field allows them to be perfect predators. Their sense of smell is fourteen times stronger than that of humans.

As with all cats, Trooper's curiosity seemed endless, and he used his heightened senses to help him explore. The entire house required investigation, and he often waited for me to join him in that duty. Every closet, cabinet, and piece of furniture had to pass a smell test. We assumed everything met with his approval, as we never noticed him avoiding a particular object. I often wondered how much information his little brain could retain from smell alone. Likewise, everything in our yard demanded examination. Trees, plants, stones, and flowers were checked each time he passed by. Special attention was given to flowers, which he seemed to enjoy.

A good nap always followed this routine. We had purchased a comfortable cat bed, which he promptly rejected, selecting instead our luxurious living room couch. But that piece of furniture was more than just a place to sleep; it also became a favorite scratching object. While lying on his back on the floor, Trooper would often pull himself along the length of the couch by sinking his claws into the bottom edge. He'd scoot along from one end to the other, flip himself over, and reverse direction. I made a slight attempt to discourage the practice by demonstrating how much fun it was to use his carpet tree, but he preferred the couch, and we had to accept the fact that it must be sacrificed for his pleasure.

Food, as we expected, was paramount in Trooper's life. No doubt the memory of going for extended periods between meals in the wild was locked in his mind. We provided him with dry food and fresh water around the clock. We let him sample a variety of wet food until he decided that chopped chicken was his favorite, with beef as a close second. That first year we found no evidence that he killed birds or any small animals. (That activity would come later, when we relocated to a ranch.) Trooper guarded his eating area with serious concern if we had visitors. Whenever the doorbell rang, he'd rush to the kitchen from wherever he was and block his food with his body. "People don't eat cat food," I tried to reassure him, but he wasn't taking any chances.

It was another story with human food, however. As a rule, everything Chi cooks smells delicious and inviting. The first time Trooper sampled spaghetti, he used his paw to lift a long noodle from my plate. "No," I scolded him softly as I prepared a small plate for him and placed it next to mine. Next his head disappeared into the salad bowl. Again, I placed a small amount on his plate and discovered it was the French dressing that had tempted him. From then on we permitted him to smell our food, but insisted he eat from his own plate on the floor. Gradually he lost interest in human food, except for fried chicken. While some might be critical of our dinner experiments, Chi and I thought they were a good way to show Trooper that he was a member of our family and to learn a little discipline in the process.

Summer passed. Trooper was now almost five months old and had gained weight, yet none of it was fat. He seemed to be all muscle and fur. We had to enlarge the cat door for a second time.

His curiosity peaked one day when I came home with a fax machine. This electronic marvel was something new at the time, and we invested in it to speed communication with our gift shop suppliers. Our early model fed thermo paper from a roll, which could be problematic, we learned, if the paper was exposed to sunlight, heat, or moisture.

We still don't know why Trooper became fascinated with the fax machine. Perhaps the buzzing sound it produced or the fact that we placed it on the kitchen floor until we could decide on a permanent location attracted him. I forgot that anything on the floor becomes the property of a cat.

The next day, Chi called for me to come to the kitchen. "Look at that!" she said, pointing to Trooper's water bowl.

In it a fax letter floated. Once exposed to water, the print had completely disappeared and the fax was unreadable. So much for speeding up communication with our suppliers! Trooper had removed the letter from the machine, and as he had done with Yellow Bear, decided to feed and water it. Two days later, the machine chime sounded and Trooper sprang to it. While eating dinner, we watched him remove the paper and head towards his bowls. I caught him a moment before the paper hit the water.

A month later we invested in a new invention, a "plain paper" (or, the current letter-type paper) machine, and no longer feared the loss of important messages. The cat showed no interest in the new machine, perhaps because it did not make the buzz sound and lacked the pleasant chime announcing the arrival of a letter.

Three additional months passed, and it had come time to visit Doctor Marg for Trooper's checkup. After quite a struggle to get him into his travel crate, Chi and I loaded him into the car for the brief journey to the hospital. But before I started the engine, my wife hit me with a strange question.

"Did you read about the big cat?" she asked.

"What big cat?"

"It's here in the morning *Review-Journal.* I brought it for you to read."

I quickly read the article, which told of an eight-year-old girl reporting to her father that a "big kitty" was sleeping under the family car in the driveway. The father took his daughter by the hand and led her outside. There he froze. Stretched out on the driveway, enjoying the morning sun, was a mountain lion. They quickly returned to the safety of the house and phoned 911.

Police officers, news teams, animal control agents, and representatives from the US Department of Wildlife flooded to the yard to see this unusual visitor to Las Vegas. The lion was tranquilized, examined at the nearby wildlife hospital, and then released high in the wooded Spring Mountains west of town. Mountain lions, mostly young ones recently separated from their mothers, have occasionally visited the suburbs of Las Vegas but neither cat nor humans have ever been harmed.

When I started the car, Trooper began to growl and his crate rocked until we reached the hospital.

During the short trip I thought of how relieved I was to be caring for a young bobcat and not a cougar. My kitty was at least a manageable weight and size.

Las Vegas water comes mostly from Lake Mead, which was created in the 1930s when the Colorado River met the newly constructed Hoover Dam.

Throughout the eighties and early nineties, there appeared to be enough water, generated by heavy snowfall far to the north, to satisfy the needs of a rapidly growing Las Vegas population. During the latter half of the nineties, people began to notice that the white marks left by receding water on canyon walls were sinking lower, and fast. The water was disappearing.

To offset the impending danger of running out of water, the Clark County Water Authority embarked on a water conservation program to save billions of gallons. In an aggressive rebate program, property owners were paid for every square foot of lawn that was converted to desert landscaping of gravel, sand, colorful stones, and native desert plants. Contractors for new homes were discouraged from planting grass after 2004. The plan worked and Las Vegas continued its fantastic growth, without new grass.

Before 2004, home builders, contractors, and landscape companies imported not only grass, but truckloads of plants, flowers, trees, bushes, and just about anything green to decorate the new homes. Naturally, a variety of small creatures who had homes in that greenery traveled along and were soon discovered by people's pets.

I have been asked why Trooper didn't hiss at anything. Well, he did. I simply failed to mention the fact in the first edition of this book.

His days of heavy hissing lasted a short time. It occurred mostly when he was a young, chubby kitten, still exploring his territory. He frequently discovered enemies, both real and imagined.

All cats hiss, some more than others. Males can become especially vocal, hissing loudly when confronting another cat. It is their best method of letting something know they are unhappy about, even fearful of, the current situation. The hiss is a warning. Whatever the cat has encountered should back away because his next act may come rapidly. That could, in a situation serious to the cat, move on to an attack with claws, then teeth.

A young cat encountering things he is unfamiliar with can go through a stage of hissing until he is comfortable and feels he has made it clear that he is much tougher than he may look.

My first experience with Trooper hissing caught me by surprise. We were in our front yard and Trooper was enjoying a little flower bed next to the house. He was about twelve weeks old at the time and still somewhat tubby. My attention was drawn to the flowerbed by a clear sound of hissing. The cat was in his attack position, ears back, hair bristling along the center of his body, his short tail slowly twitching left to right.

I rushed to him, fearing he had encountered something dangerous, perhaps a rattlesnake. But, there, only a few feet away, was a very ugly looking frog; at least, judging by the length of his hind legs, he had to be a frog.

As could be expected, the frog suddenly hopped a short distance from the flowers to the grass. The hissing had worked. The enemy was moving away.

The cat followed the frog, hissing with each of its jumps. This had become an intriguing game for the cat, although it was not especially appreciated by the frog. But I quickly became concerned. Was the frog poisonous?

I scooped up my kitten before he could physically attack the creature, and carried the squirming feline into the house.

Fortunately, cats, especially young ones, can become easily distracted. Once inside, Trooper instantly found a new threat and began hissing at the rice cooker. Then it was the electric can opener. Thus began his hissing fit, which continued for a few days until he had made it understood that he was in command of his little world. All threatening items had been neutralized by the hissing.

I never saw the frog again. I'm sure it found a safer territory in which to hop.

CHAPTER 5

Getting to Know You

"Time spent with cats is never wasted."

Sigmund Freud

"TROOPER IS AT FIFTEEN POUNDS," Doctor Marg stated during his checkup. "He's a little more than half grown and appears to be in excellent health. Do you have any questions regarding his condition? Is there anything worrying you?"

"No, not really," I replied. "He's strong, and runs and jumps as I expected. But, I wonder about his legs."

"What's wrong with his legs? Have you noticed a lump or . . . ?"

"No," I interrupted. "He's short compared to bobcats I have seen in photos."

The doctor smiled, and for a moment, dodged my statement. "The nurses are playing with Trooper in the exam room," she said. "He truly enjoys human attention. This is a pleasant surprise. Did you notice the man wearing a white shirt waiting in the reception area?"

"Yes."

"He is much taller than you are, yet you are both white American males around the same age. Every species is built differently, including bobcats. Do you recall your concern about Trooper's rounded ears when you first brought him to me? Look at those ears now—they're large, pointed, and erect. Trooper will grow a little taller. Be thankful he doesn't get much larger. I'm sure he is difficult to handle already. Does he let you pick him up and carry him about?"

"Not very easily," I admitted. "I can pick him up, but if I try to carry him very far he kicks and squirms and makes funny whirring sounds. Luckily, he doesn't use his claws on me. He saves those for his kitty tree and the couch."

Doctor Marg chuckled. "How about scratch marks on trees outside?"

"Oh, yes. There are plenty of those."

"He's marking his territory with the scent from his paws," she explained. "Another cat will know his size by the height of the scratch marks. I'm curious. How do you discipline him? Does he respond to your commands?"

"Like with a human child, it's been a bit of a learning curve for both of us. Of course, I never strike him, or even act like I intend to."

"Good!" she heartily approved.

"I don't shout at him either. I simply say 'no' in a firm voice."

"And he responds positively?"

"Yes. Well, most of the time. I think he always knows exactly what I want. He often looks at me as if waiting for my response."

"Hmm . . . interesting. Has he learned the meaning of any words yet?"

"Yes. You'll see a list of words he understands in my log. I'm leaving a copy for you. He's developing a nice vocabulary."

"Wonderful," she smiled. "And it includes the command, 'no'?"

"He also responds when I say his name in a sharp tone. So, he seems to understand the importance of tone as much as the actual word. After we correct him we give him lots of love and attention by stroking his head and back. He follows us about the house, observing what we do. He wants to be involved."

"What you describe sounds like a normal domestic cat. I'm pleased, and a little surprised he is behaving like one. Do you think, at this point, he believes he is human? So many owners say that about their pet."

"Not at all," I reported. "He thinks I'm a cat, just not a very capable one. I can't jump up on a wall, I'm not very fast on my feet, and my tree climbing abilities are nonexistent."

The doctor leaned back in her chair and laughed. "Well, you're growing up together," she said. "That will form a good bond between the two of you. By the way, you'll soon notice his coat becoming thicker. Winter will be here in a few weeks. As with all animals, it's not only the changing temperature, but the position of the sun affecting their fur. Trooper's body doesn't know he'll have a warm house to sleep in this winter."

During our visit with Doctor Marg, I learned that Trooper's physical and blood test results proved him to be a healthy young bobcat. Very much relieved, we returned home in time for my afternoon nap, which I usually enjoyed on the living room carpet.

Up until this point, Trooper had neither been a lap cat nor had he enjoyed being cuddled. His affection towards me was limited to purring when petted. So what happened next on that October afternoon came as a happy surprise.

As I awoke from my nap, I became aware of some kind of weight on my right leg, just below the knee. I lifted myself up on my elbow and saw that Trooper had fallen asleep with his head on my leg and his front paws wrapped around my calf. To say that I was excited would be an understatement; I was utterly thrilled! This animal, who had been totally wild a few months earlier, had begun to express not only his affection, but his trust.

After a few moments, I asked him a silly question. "Are you awake?" He opened his eyes, stared at me, then stood, stretched, and walked towards the cat door as if nothing unusual had occurred. Guess he was awake after all.

We repeated this sleeping position over the next several days, then I decided to try something different. I lay on my back, extended my arm with my palm facing upward, and promptly fell asleep. I awoke with my cat's head resting in my hand. The next day he cuddled next to me, using my arm as a pillow. From that day on, whenever we napped together, his snuggling position was the same. I had replaced Yellow Bear as his sleeping companion.

Winter neared and Trooper's coat changed. Soon he resembled the fuzzy bobcat we saw in pictures. My skinny little cat had grown considerably, enough so that we enlarge his cat door once again, and yet one more time a few weeks later.

Each day, I was reminded by Trooper's behavior that I had a most unusual cat. As expected, he had become very protective of not only his food, but also of what he considered his territory, which at the time was only our small yard. This protection also extended to Chi and myself. He would growl if someone came near us until we assured him all was safe. Yet he was still young, and if the situation appeared threatening, he simply disappeared, but not completely. I learned that he remained nearby in some special hiding place, watching from a crouched position, ready to attack if necessary. It's true: to be a good protector, one needs practice.

One morning as Chi and I prepared to go out, Trooper rushed past us and out the front doorway as if on a special mission. He suddenly stopped, looked back at us, and then flattened himself on the sidewalk with his four legs sticking out

"What the hell is he doing?" I exclaimed. I was answered with a strange, shaking sensation. For a second or two, my head felt as if I had consumed too many shots of bourbon.

"Earthquake!" Chi announced. "Very far away." (As it turned out, the epicenter of the quake was near Los Angeles.) My Japanese wife knew instantly what we were experiencing. People living in Japan grow up feeling quakes routinely. To them it is an expected part of life.

Trooper remained low to the ground for a few more seconds, then he stood and walked slowly towards the house.

"He knew something was about to happen before we felt anything," I said.

"Animals always feel the quake first," she replied. "Oh, look!" she added, pointing towards two women across the street. They were walking with a cat. "Isn't that cute? I wonder if Trooper would stay near us if we went for a walk together."

"I doubt it," I answered. "We never . . ."

"No, Trooper!" she interrupted.

Before we could stop him, Trooper dashed across the street and slammed himself into the cat. With all the screaming that followed, from both the women and the cats, I feared I would find the other cat severely injured. I rushed across the street and somehow managed to lift Trooper away from the battle. I apologized to the women and discovered with relief that their cat did not appear to be hurt. Neither did Trooper, but fur from both cats was floating in the air. "Take that big bully home!" one lady shouted at me.

"Yes, ma'am! I'm very sorry. It will never happen again. Your cat appears to be okay."

"He's not hurt," she replied with anger, "he's frightened. We all are!"

I carried a squirming Trooper to our yard and gave him a harsh scolding. "You must not attack other cats! This is your territory, over here!" I waved my hand in a circular motion as if covering our entire front yard.

He understood by my tone of voice that I was not pleased, but I'm sure he could not grasp the reason. In the days to come, I observed him watching people as they walked their dogs and, once in a while, a cat. But I didn't see him launch another attack.

I had started thinking that it might be a good time to relocate. We needed inventory storage room for our growing business, and our cat needed space to be himself. We had been looking into some small ranch properties for sale on the south end of town. Some were actually in the desert and appeared to be perfect for our needs. Trooper would have lots of room to explore. We then prepared to place our house on the market.

I've learned from browsing the Internet, especially from Facebook groups, that most cat owners report bizarre behavior from their pets. Trooper was no exception. There was one episode, in particular, which we shall never forget.

One afternoon, shortly after a nap, Chi and I were working at the kitchen table when Trooper bolted in with what appeared to be a piece of wood in his mouth. He proceeded directly to his dinner bowl and dropped the object on the dry food. I moved closer to learn the identity of the treasure.

But it turned out not to be a piece of wood, but the mummified remains of a small bird with which he now shared a meal, normally reserved for Yellow Bear. After a few moments on the pile of dry food, the mummy bird received a dip in the water bowl. Then the cat snatched it in his mouth and carried it to the top of his cat tree.

We watched silently, wrapped in curiosity. What did the cat plan to do?

Suddenly, with a quick jerk of his head, Trooper flung the mummy bird into the air. It fell directly to the floor with a dull thump. Trooper stared at the bird for more than a minute, then brought it back to his food and water bowls for another dunking. With the bird in his mouth, he sprang up the cat tree to toss it in the air once again. Sadly, it fell with the same dull sound. If he was trying to make the bird fly again, Trooper's experiment with resurrection surely failed. He yowled from the top of his tree. Finally he climbed down, picked the bird up in his mouth, and disappeared with it through the cat door. We never saw the mummy bird again, but I was left wondering what this cat had been thinking.

Skeptics will say that a cat cannot think or plan; that an animal only behaves by instinct. These same skeptics would say Trooper had been playing a game with his mummy bird. Cat owners, of course, might argue differently, and propose a hypothesis something along the lines of what I came up with to explain this strange episode.

True, I had seen Trooper feed and water Yellow Bear, but I think he did that out of affection, not as a wish for resurrection. He had never seen a live Yellow Bear, and there were no others in his world to compare it to. Yellow Bear could not be expected to fly or walk or sing because it never had before.

However, birds were different. They are supposed to fly and sing. Trooper had seen them do this every day he lived with us. Perhaps he thought that if he provided food and water, then the bird would come back to life. If this were truly his intention, then I felt a little sad for Trooper. After this experiment, did he now realize that death is final? How could I expect a simple animal to comprehend this when we humans, with our vast intellect, have such difficulty accepting a final fate?

Of course, I cannot say with any certainty what my young cat had been thinking during his experiment. But I had learned that despite his lineage, Trooper was sensitive with a sweet disposition. His curiosity seemed to reach beyond that of other cats I would meet in later years, or perhaps it was simply different, for he often combined this trait with some sort of experiment.

Unfortunately, in the years to come, Trooper would witness death many times and eventually be forced to face the animal that had killed his feline family. On that day of the mummy bird I decided it was time to become more involved with Trooper's play. I planned to introduce him to little fuzzy toys which, some day at our new ranch, would be replaced with live animals.

CHAPTER 6

Games We Cats Play

"In nine lifetimes you'll never know as much about your cat as your cat knows about you."

Michel de Montaigne

They descended upon Las Vegas in wave upon wave of noise. News broadcasts on television announced their arrival all day and into the late evening. They quickly became the subject of conversation around Las Vegas. No, I'm not talking about tourists—well, not exactly. These visitors were cicadas, buzzing insects welcomed only by birds who would enjoy endless meals for a few days, even though their constant feasting didn't make a dent in the bugs' population. Fortunately, these insects were harmless to all creatures, great and small, but they were annoying nonetheless.

I returned home late one afternoon and noticed my neighbor working in his flower bed next to their driveway.

"What's that buzzing noise?" I asked.

He mopped his brow with a shirt sleeve, "Cicadas. They started that racket a few hours ago. My dog has already eaten a handful of 'em."

"Make him sick?"

"No. According to the news, they won't make pets sick." I was somewhat relieved to learn that I had no worries about Trooper eating one of those bugs, but I didn't really expect him to be interested in insects. I entered my house and found my wife waiting for me in the kitchen. "Your big cat is having a great time catching bugs," she announced jokingly. "He's been busy at it all afternoon. That's what we have, a bug-catching cat!"

Trooper was lying on the floor at the open glass door with his front legs outstretched. A high-pitched buzzing sound indicated there must be a bug trapped under his paws.

"He catches the bugs," Chi explained, "bats them around the floor. Then he takes them outside and releases them. They fly away."

I lay down next to Trooper, my face near his paws. "That's a very nice bug," I said to the cat.

He sat up and answered me with a crunching sound. No more bug.

I watched as the cat trotted across the little bridge and into the backyard. Suddenly he leaped into the air and snatched a bug with his paws. It was still buzzing when he placed it in front of me and pushed it close to my face.

"Thank you, Trooper," I said graciously. "You're a good hunter. This is a wonderful bug!"

He seemed pleased with my compliments, and trotted back to the yard for more hunting.

"Are you going to eat it now, or save it for later?" my wife asked teasingly.

"I'll wrap it up and you can toss it out the front door. I don't want him to see you do it. I might disappoint him."

Trooper became totally involved in hunting cicadas from this point forward. I never knew exactly how many he devoured during those two weeks before they vanished and the air was silent once again. (In fact, we wouldn't see the cicadas for another seventeen years.)

A few days later I heard a car horn in front of our house and looked out the window. A large white van had parked there and printed on its side were large red letters that read PRETTY PAWS HOME PET GROOMING.

"Chi! Did you order some kind of pet grooming service?" I yelled.

"Yes!" she answered from the bedroom. "That cat has been with us for a few months and he hasn't had a bath. He hates to travel so I thought he would be more comfortable with a bath here."

"Is he supposed to get a bath? I thought cats clean themselves."

Before she could answer, we were interrupted by the doorbell. When I opened the door, a man stood before me wearing a blue cap, matching colored jumpsuit, and sporting a black, well-trimmed goatee. The embroidered logo on jumpsuit assured me he was from "Pretty Paws" and had come to give my cat a bath.

"Are you Johnson?" the man said sharply.

"Yes. Come in."

Trooper, who had been sleeping atop his kitchen cat tree, was now awake and alert, his large ears pointed forward.

The man then shouted, "Well! Where's the cat?"

Before I could answer, Trooper replied with an ear-piercing scream, followed by a deep growl.

"That's the cat," I said.

"You gotta be joking . . ." the man mumbled. "Forget about it," he said as he turned and marched back to his van.

Trooper leaped to the floor, rushed out the back door, and disappeared into the safety of the bamboo grove. There was no time to stop and guard the food bowl. I laughed as I thought, who was more afraid of whom—the cat or the groomer? Battle of the species, indeed.

Except for being trapped in an occasional rainstorm (occasional is a good description for Las Vegas as the city only receives three to four inches of rain each year), that day was the closest our cat ever came to a bath. He, like all his wild cousins, groomed himself and never smelled offensive, at least as far as I could tell. Of course, he had no idea as to the purpose of the man's visit. He simply didn't like the tone of his voice. Once the cat was certain the man had departed, he returned to the kitchen, only to be greeted by another disruption to his routine.

"What's that?" I asked as Chi removed a leather harness from a shopping bag.

"It's a kitty halter, size large. He might choke with a collar if he got it caught on something. I have a long retractable leash. Now you can take him for a walk."

"Great idea, but I don't think he's going to like this. We'll give it a try. Come on, Troop; Mama has a gift for you."

He smelled the leather and started to walk away, but I held him while Chi slipped the harness over his head and managed to buckle the straps at his chest. At first, he thought we were playing one of our wrestling games, but soon realized this was something different. I knew that the moment I released him we would witness a wild reaction.

"Okay," I said to Chi. "Back up slowly. I'm going to turn him loose."

I wasn't wrong. We were in for quite a show. Trooper first rushed to the couch in the living room, bounced from it to the fireplace mantel, then to the coffee table, from which he slinked to the floor and started rolling in an effort to free himself of that horrible thing gripping his body. Finally he ran to me and lay flat at my feet, his eyes pleading for help while he whimpered.

We had been successful, thus far, in domesticating our wild cat, but I had pushed my luck this time. I carefully removed the harness while stroking his back with the palm of my hand. He responded by purring contentedly. In the future, walks would strictly be decided by the cat.

The harness was not his only objection to certain types of domestication. I learned, as many cat owners do, not to rub his chest or belly. Some cats love that kind of attention, but others react quickly to protect this sensitive and vulnerable part of their body. This is especially true for wild cats. If Trooper rolled over on his back and exposed his underside, it signified two things: Either he trusted me, or he was setting a trap to lure me into destruction. For us, the tummy rub became a game of mutual trust. The cat learned that I intended no harm. When I touched his chest or stomach, he instantly seized my arm with his front paws and clamped his jaws down near my elbow. At the same moment, he would kick me with his rear legs. His teeth never broke my skin unless I jerked, which I admittedly did the first few times. I still have scars to remind me of my lack of trust. He seemed amused to play this game. Somehow he knew just how much pressure to apply to my arm without breaking my skin.

One morning Chi called me into the living room. I stumbled in, still half asleep.

"Look at that!" she said, pointing to a wadded candy bar wrapper lying in the center of the floor.

"Don't blame me!" I responded. "Where did it come from?"

"Your cat brought it in."

"That's silly! Why would he bring that thing in here?"

"Every morning for the past two weeks there has been something different at the same spot. He's bringing in trash from the street during the night."

"He wants us to find it, doesn't he? I wonder why."

"I think so," she said. "The first few days I tossed the stuff into the garbage, but then I decided to save it and think logically. What is he thinking? Go look on the kitchen counter at the box of stuff." She had marked the box with a felt-tipped pen: "Trooper's Treasures." It contained an odd assortment of chewing gum wrappers, a bottle cap, crushed soda and beer cans, a plastic coffee cup, a piece of rubber from a tire, half of a cigar, and, the strangest of all, a twelve-inch piece of rope tied with a number of strands of clear plastic fishing line. Despite its seeming oddity, it became a very special possession. "Rope," as we called it, was fed and watered like Yellow Bear, and Trooper began carrying it about, introducing "rope" to his world.

If we said, "Go find rope," or "Where is rope?" he would retrieve it from a hiding place and walk about with it in his mouth. Unlike a dog, he never fetched it to us; he only proved he knew rope's location.

The trash gathering continued until we moved to the ranch, which we had been planning to do for some time. With an unending assortment of things and places to investigate at the new property, his trash gathering ceased. Rope, however, retained a special place in his life for years. Some days he carried it about the house and property, and then it disappeared, only to be retrieved a day or so later.

Trooper had another box filled with a variety of kitty toys. Like many cats, he was more interested in climbing in and out of the box than actually playing with toys. It finally occurred to me that he didn't know what the small, fuzzy creatures were for. Apparently he had never seen a live mouse, or didn't recognize the similarities.

I selected a dozen little toy mice from the box. The cat watched as I carefully arranged them in a military formation and began to move them forward as if they were marching towards an objective. I lay on the floor and was quickly joined by the cat, who at first appeared interested in the game.

"Now watch, Trooper," I firmly said. "First line is for the tough soldiers. The next line we move up slowly because they're the reinforcements."

My wife watched the experiment, covering her mouth to hide a laugh. She quietly slipped out of the room.

Trooper studied the mice and watched as I scooted the toys about, simulating a fight sequence. After a few minutes, it was then his chance to join the game. He first smacked at several mice with his paw, then picked one up by its tail and carried it outside to the bamboo grove. He returned, seized another mouse, and joined it with the first one. This continued until he had relocated all the mice.

"What happened to your game?" Chi inquired as she reentered the room to check on our progress.

"I'm not sure. He has his own ideas."

"Where are all the mice?"

"He carried them outside."

The next morning we woke to discover the mice scattered helter-skelter across the living room floor. The cat had returned them. After that, he showed very little interest in the fuzzy toys no matter how much I tried to interact with him. The goldfish swimming in the pond were far more of an attraction and spending time observing them apparently was more important than playing with toys. In time, as with all children, cats or people, his interest would change.

But it was in the backyard that I made an interesting discovery: Cats don't know that humans can't see in the dark. Of course, cats cannot see in total darkness, but in the desert, or forest, it is never totally dark. There is always some light from the moon and stars. Even on a cloudy night, there is reflection from the clouds, and it provides enough to aid the night creature's visibility. The night belongs to the cat. Felines have predatory instincts and their vision in dim light aids their survival. If given the opportunity, cats will hunt shortly before dawn and just after sunset when the light is not so dim or bright. The creatures the cat hunts during those hours also have good vision in dim light, but alas, we humans have limited visual ability.

To prove my theory, one crisp winter evening, I decided to walk along the gravel path that wound its way a short distance through our backyard. I moved slowly as it was very dark while searching intently for Trooper. Suddenly something smashed against my left leg, almost knocking me off balance. There had been no sound. I could not see what hit me. It was as if someone had thrown an invisible football with a powerful arm.

Certain the aggressor was Trooper, my eyes strained to see him. No luck.

I took two more steps and the strike came again, this time against my right leg. And again, not a sound.

"Trooper!" I called.

No response.

"Trooper! Where are you?"

The reply was a whirring sound as the cat neared.

"Come on! Let's go inside!" I called to him, and he trotted beside me to the warmth of the kitchen.

So albeit unwittingly, I had participated in a new game for Trooper. A few nights following, it became fun to guess which leg would be hit as he rushed at me, silent in the darkness. I thought about how I might match his surprise attack capabilities. Of course, we humans must resort to scientific equipment to accomplish such things. This need led me to a gun show at the Las Vegas Convention Center the following weekend.

To me, the interesting thing about gun shows aren't the guns, but the odd assortment of other items sometimes only remotely related to guns, like beef jerky, T-shirts, jewelry, and antiques. I moved directly to a table loaded with an impressive assortment of obsolete Russian military gear, including night vision equipment.

A man standing next to me remarked, "Funny. For a million years no one could see in the dark. Look at this crowd! Now everyone wants to see in the dark!"

His comment rang with an element of truth. I found exactly what I wanted: a cheap, first-generation scope that resembled a bulky pair of field binoculars. It was battery powered, used the light from stars (or any available light for that matter), and had an infrared beam that was activated by simply pushing a button. This was perfect for my use.

I rushed home with my purchase and waited patiently for darkness to capture the desert, anxious to try my new hi-tech equipment. "Now, Mister Cat, we are going to be equal," I mumbled determinedly, before traveling into the backyard and activating my new toy. A slightly greenish, fuzzy image appeared before my eyes. I pushed the infrared button and the image became clearer. But where was the cat?

I scanned the yard, pushing the infrared button, and then remembered he had to be looking directly at me for his eyes to reflect the beam. Suddenly I saw him. He was crouching low in the bamboo grove, his favorite hiding place. I began to walk slowly along the path, pretending I did not know his location. I turned slightly, keeping the cat in sight with my equipment.

Without a sound, Trooper sprang to the top of the block wall, crept a short distance, then dropped to the ground. He was about eighteen feet away as he silently struck the earth.

Crouching low, he began to flit from shadow to shadow, always keeping the bushes between us. Now, for the first time, I realized the stealth of a cat as he moved. He calculated the placement of each paw as he moved closer and closer, preparing for a rush attack. The cat knew every inch of his territory and what would most benefit his stalking. For a complete surprise, his final rush must be very short so that his prey had little or no time to react. If he were really hunting, he would strike at the back or side of his prey, aiming his bite for the neck, just below the skull. Of course, stalking me was only a game. His brush against my leg was the same as a *touché* in fencing.

I turned off my equipment and let him attack. As before, he quickly disappeared into the darkness afterwards.

I went into the house to prepare for bed and closed the louvered double doors to our room behind me.

"Did your new toy work?" my wife quietly inquired as I climbed into bed.

"Oh, yes," I answered. "I learned so many things. Did you realize that cats don't know we can't see in the dark as they do? They stalk and use the moonlight shadows for concealment, thinking we might see them."

"I never thought about it," she replied. "I always . . ."

We were interrupted by a crashing sound. The louvered doors rattled.

"What was that?" she exclaimed, sitting up in bed.

"Don't know. Something is trying to force the doors open." My response was followed by another crashing sound at the door. I wasn't frightened as I figured it had to be my cat.

Then, one of the doors swung open with Trooper holding the handle lever. He had learned he could not force the door open by smashing into it. So he tried, with success, to use the handle, just as we did. His weight, then about twenty pounds, was enough to push the latch and swing the door open.

"You belong on the couch," Chi said to the cat. His answer was to curl up on the bed at our feet.

"I guess he's tired of sleeping alone," I whispered. "We play together and eat together. Now we sleep together."

Trooper began to purr. In a minute there was silence. He had fallen asleep. It was strange how the presence of this once wild animal gave us a comfortable, secure feeling.

CHAPTER 7

Tough Guy

"What greater gift than the love of a cat."

Charles Dickens

THE DESERT ENVIRONS WHERE WE lived was slowly disappearing as rows of new tract homes, all of similar size, design, and shape, and in a row, began dotting the landscape. Even the ravine where I had found Trooper a few months earlier felt the leveling blades of earth-moving equipment.

One Sunday morning, while there was no construction going on, I decided to hike over to the ravine and see that part of the desert one last time. I confess that I was being sentimental and desired to visit the spot where my cat and I were first united before it, too, disappeared.

But I was too late. The ravine had become a concrete canal used to control the flow of water through a culvert under a nearby road, and on to the Colorado River, miles away. That day it was dry, but it was built to handle the flash floods that would inevitably come in the rainy season.

In such a short time, everything there had changed. Dirt roads, soon to be paved, crisscrossed and circled through the desert floor where I once spent so many hours refreshing and relaxing my mind through hiking.

While lulling into my familiar meditative hiking stance, my thoughts were interrupted abruptly by a rasping scream high above me. It was followed by another scream that tapered downward. It sounded like an unusual steam whistle, but I had heard the scream before and knew it came from a red-tailed hawk.

I looked up into the clear sky to see a pair of hawks soaring above me. It was a thrill to see those large, dark brown birds with their russet-red tail feathers circling and then flapping their fifty-inch wings slowly to conserve energy. Even though they can fly at forty miles per hour, they appeared to be hovering in the air. It was truly a majestic sight.

The birds must have spotted a small rodent, rabbit, or lizard—all scrumptious snacks for hawks—because one of them banked sharply, folded its giant wings, and dove earthward. (These predators can reach speeds of over 120 miles per hour when they dive for an attack.) The other bird continued to circle overhead, only tighter while lowering its altitude. In this way it served as a backup for its diving mate.

The first bird smashed onto the ground, snatched the small animal, and lifted it by its talons into the sky. Joined by its mate, the pair flew off to enjoy their meal in private. I'm sure they could still see me as they flew away, as a hawk's eyesight is eight times that of humans. It is not surprising, I thought, that many Native American tribes consider the feathers of those magnificent birds sacred.

I walked home feeling somewhat sad that my cat's ravine had disappeared and distraught over the destruction of the desert. The more homes the developers sold, the more I dreamed of our move to a ranch, further out from the city. But that day was still a few weeks away. With these new homes came a variety of people who were relocating to Las Vegas from all parts of America. The town was growing faster than anyone, including the city's original planners, had anticipated. I would soon discover that one can meet a variety of interesting people through the friendship of a cat.

Trooper was now a young adult even though he behaved like a large kitten. According to Dr. Marg, he was now at twenty pounds, and had probably reached more than one-half his expected full-grown weight.

Even Trooper seemed concerned about our rapidly expanding neighborhood, especially the heavy trucks on our streets. During daylight hours he hid in our backyard, safely away from all the traffic, or napped near his goldfish pond. We had no idea how far he roamed at night. But it was far enough for him to meet a new kitty friend. This was a young gray cat that Trooper invited over to play. Or perhaps the gray cat had simply followed Trooper.

However it started, one day the gray cat followed Trooper through the front door to the dry food bowl in the kitchen where they enjoyed a brief snack together. Trooper made no effort to guard his food this time. Chi and I watched with interest as he led his friend into the backyard and introduced him to a variety of trees and bushes which all had to be examined with typical cat curiosity. But things changed when it came to the fish pond. Trooper made it understood, with a short growl, that the pond and its secrets were off limits.

Observing Trooper's pal, I intuited that the young cat belonged to our neighbors from three houses away. I had watched children playing with him in their front yard. Their mother seemed friendly. She often smiled and waved to me as she drove them to school.

Her husband stayed home during the day and made a grand appearance by mid-morning to work in their driveway on an old pickup truck. Other neighbors referred to him as "that tough guy" because of his large size and loud voice, which he frequently exercised by shouting obscenities at no particular target, except, perhaps, his old truck. His work clothes consisted of stained and patched jeans and an oil-spattered T-shirt. He never exhibited any anger towards his wife and children, but his deep, thunderous voice carried his vulgar words yards away, causing parents to cringe.

Tough Guy, as I inwardly christened him, worked on his truck almost daily until dinnertime, when, to the neighborhood's relief, he drove away to a night job wearing a clean T-shirt and well-fitting jeans. The next day, the truck repair began again, along with the shouting and the sound of a hammer pounding on metal. Actually, if it wasn't for all the noise, I doubt if anyone would have known Tough Guy existed.

One Saturday morning, Trooper was playing "hide and seek, chase and roll" with the gray cat in our front yard. Eventually Trooper became bored and curled up under a bush next to the house to take a nap. His gray friend joined him.

It occurred to me that Tough Guy's family might be unaware their cat was with us, so I thought it wise to let them know by introducing myself.

"Hey!" I shouted towards my neighbor as I waved my arms. "I have your kitten over here!"

Tough Guy turned away from his truck and stared at me a moment. He wiped his hands on his T-shirt and started walking in my direction.

Never wanting to miss out on my activities, Trooper crawled out from his resting place, followed by the gray cat.

In a few moments the towering figure of Tough Guy stood before me. "Were you calling me?" he asked in a deep raspy voice.

"Yes, I have your kitten here. He follows my cat around and they play together sometimes. I thought your children might miss him and worry."

Tough Guy hunched his huge shoulders and turned to look at his cat. "There you are, you stupid cat." Then he noticed Trooper and exclaimed, "Damn! What the hell kind of cat is that?"

"Oh," I answered quickly, "he was a stray. Found him a few months ago."

"Looks like some kind of wild cat, don't he?" Tough Guy observed.

"Yes," I replied, "he looks wild, but he is very tame and friendly."

"Oh," he said, and then shouted at his kitten, "Come here, you stupid ugly cat!" And, with a big hand, he reached down and scooped up the kitten. "You're more trouble than you're worth," he continued scolding. "Damn cat! If it weren't for the kids, I should break your neck! Maybe I'll do it anyway."

Men who verbally abuse their pets have always irritated me. I'm not interested in learning about their frustrations with life or their psychological problems. To abuse a creature who depends upon us for food and shelter, an animal who is helpless, is, in my opinion, an act of cowardice. I worried about the future of the gray cat, and decided to play it safe by seeing if I could convert him, even in the slightest degree. "I'm sorry. I haven't introduced myself. I'm Johnson."

To my surprise, Tough Guy held out his empty hand. "I'm Schultz. Glad to meet you. I don't know many people in this here neighborhood. I work at night, busy working on my truck most days."

"That's an interesting truck. Does it run good?"

"Needs lots of work," he said. "It don't look like much, but it gets me there."

"You are fortunate, Mr. Schultz. These days, most guys have no idea how to fix their own vehicles."

"Yeah. You can forget the mister. Just call me Schultz."

"Okay, Schultz. May I take a closer look at your kitten?"

Schultz frowned, then nodded. "Sure. I would give him to you, but he belongs to the kids. Me, I don't like cats or dogs." He ended with a laugh that sounded more like a grunt.

Ignoring his statement, I lifted one of the kitten's front legs. "Just as I thought." I exclaimed. "This is an unusual cat. He's very special. You're lucky."

"What's so special about this here cat? He's as ordinary as they come. I got him free from a guy at the shop."

I had to quickly concoct a believable story, one that the big man would accept and also ensure a safe future for the gray cat. "Free! Wow! You can't beat free, especially for a cat of this quality. I studied about cats with a local vet and learned a lot."

"Quality?"

"Well," I paused, pretending to carefully examine the kitten, "I'm not sure of his actual dollar value, but you're going to be proud of this cat."

"Why?"

"Look at these paws." I held one up for his inspection, "Feel the muscles in his leg. He's young now, but he's going to grow up to be a very strong cat."

"You think so?"

"Yes," I continued, knowing I had his attention. "Look at these erect ears and those eyes. Did you know he can see 180 degrees?"

"What's that mean?"

"It means, he may be looking at you, but he can see something slipping up on him, to the left or right, from the corner of his eyes. We can't do that."

"Yeah, that's for sure," Schultz chuckled.

"Feel his fur! This is special fur. God designed it to attract the sun during the winter to keep him warm. It'll keep him cool during our hot summers."

"Well," Schultz said with a grin. "I ain't gonna argue with God."

"This cat will grow up to be plenty smart," I assured him. "He already respects you. He's going to give you lots of love."

"That's silly."

"No, not silly," I said. "You know Charles Dickens?"

"Charles Dickens?" Schultz appeared to be in deep thought. "Sure! You mean old Charlie at the Six Gun Café down at the corner?"

"No," I laughed. "A different Charles Dickens. The famous English writer. You know what he said?"

"No, what?"

"He said, 'What greater gift than the love of a cat.'"

Schultz laughed deeply. "He got famous for saying that?"

"No. He's famous for writing stories like *A Christmas Carol*. You know, the story about Scrooge."

"I saw the movie," Schultz announced. "Scrooge was a mean dude until a bunch of ghosts showed him around. Then he became a nice guy, kind of generous."

"Exactly!" I complimented. "Dickens believed that the love from a cat is a wonderful thing. And that's what you've got. I don't know why, but this cat loves you. He may save your life someday."

"You think so, huh?"

"Sure do. Every now and then we read in the paper where a cat wakes up the family when their house is on fire."

Schultz began to stroke the kitten's head, who responded with a strong purr.

"See there," I said. "He's purring for you. Means that he loves and respects you."

"Guess he is a pretty good cat." Schultz nodded his neckless head.

"Sure, he's good and smart. You have been working so hard you never had time to notice him. Your kids discovered how smart this cat is, I'm sure."

"Yeah. Them kids are smart." Schultz held out his hand while cuddling the kitten to his chest with the other. "Well," he said, "thanks Johnson. You come visit sometime. I want to learn more about this here cat of mine."

"I'll do that, Schultz."

"Come on cat," he said. "We gotta get home. Time for lunch."

When Schultz and his cat reached the end of the driveway, he turned and waved. "Thanks again!" The kitten was staring at me from the man's massive shoulder. It might have been my imagination, but I thought I saw the cat wink at me as they walked away. My promotional pitch had only played a small part in converting Schultz. The kitten's purring at just the right moment had sealed the deal. Either way, that kitten and I now had a new friend. At least I hoped that would be the case.

A few days after my conversation with Schultz, a couple who were out for a morning walk stopped by to tell me that they had passed Tough Guy's house and saw him holding his gray cat. They were surprised when Schultz told them how special his pet was. "Guess no one is going to argue with Tough Guy," the neighbor said, "but that cat sure looked ordinary to me."

I smiled. "If he says that cat is special, maybe it is, at least to him."

About a week before we were to move to our new home, I walked over to visit Schultz. He was busy installing a new mirror on the passenger side of his truck. We talked a few moments, and as I turned to go, I noticed his gray cat asleep inside the truck.

"Looks like you got a friend there," I said.

"Yeah," replied Schultz. "He thinks he's my helper, but really he sleeps most of the time."

A warm feeling of success came over me. I knew then I was successful. Tough Guy and his cat were friends and as his "helper" the cat's future as a member of the family was complete and guaranteed. I had worked on the hunch that even tough guys can have a soft side. Finding it and working with that side is the key. The cat provided the key.

CHAPTER 8

We Move

"Letting the cat out of the bag is a whole lot easier than putting it back in."

Will Rogers

To get Trooper into his travel crate required a lot of energy and luck. I knew he associated the crate with a trip to the vet, since he had never been anywhere else in it. Even though he was peaceful when with Doctor Marg, like most cats, he didn't cherish a trip anywhere.

If the cat saw us preparing the crate, a great disappearing act quickly followed. Even in our small house, and considering his size, he still found inventive places to hide. An old cat-luring trick, a plate of tuna fish, didn't work. But human intelligence and determination eventually won and we carried the unhappy friend to his crate. But that was the easy part; getting him into the crate brought great frustration for us all.

To avoid being lowered into the crate, he activated his first defense by extending four legs, rendering his flat body impossible to push in. His deep growls would have been enough to discourage a

54

normal person from further attempts, but we knew this to be only a bluff. And it was impossible to push him in through the front, gate-like door. The larger door at the top presented the only possibility. Here, with considerable effort, we were finally successful.

Once inside he usually remained quiet for a few moments as if contemplating his situation. Did we plan to release him? Convinced that possibility did not exist, things changed quickly. The crate would shake for a minute as he tested its strength by kicking the sides. Then the growling and yowling began, which tapered off to a variety of complaining sounds, mostly cries of different volume.

On that day we were moving from our little house to "ranch property" south of Las Vegas, far away from the casinos and bright lights so familiar to most visitors. This was at a time when the Vegas real estate business was really healthy. Our home had sold quickly and with a nice profit, enabling us to make a substantial down payment on the small ranch.

With Trooper securely in his crate I carried him to my car. Before we could enter, my "Tough" friend, Schultz, came to say goodbye.

"I'd seen the moving van and guessed you would be leaving today," he said. Then he gave me an interesting bit of information.

"By the way, I should tell you . . . I named my cat Dickens."

"Dickens?" I was puzzled.

"Yes. After the writer guy who said something about a gift of love from a cat. You told me that story."

"Oh, Charles Dickens," I responded eagerly. "Dickens is a great name for your cat."

"You think so?"

"Yes, for sure!"

"Well, Johnson," Schultz said while shaking my hand, "You come see me and Dickens sometime. And bring that big, wild-looking cat of yours!"

"You bet I will, Schultz."

And with that goodbye, Trooper and I entered the car and headed to our new home.

The ranch property spread over almost five acres and included a three-bedroom home, a pool, a guest house, and a separate one-level building that would serve as our office and warehouse. A circular driveway ran between rows of Italian cypress trees to a sheltered front porch, and then continued on to connect to an old, seldom-used country road. The abundance of trees, bushes, and desert plants dotting the land presented a perfect playground for Trooper.

The nearest home to the south was almost seven hundred yards away, with nothing but desert in between. A gully, flush with small trees, creosote bushes, and a variety of sweet-smelling sage-brush separated our property from that desert area.

To the west, directly across the road, was more desert, bordered by homes along the south and north edge. Those homeowners, I was informed by the realtor, often had horses that were safe within white rail fencing. Those ranches were four hundred yards from our front door. On our north side, stretching a mile to a highway, lay an abandoned golf course known as "Fairway to the Stars," once owned by band leader and all-around entertainer, Louis Prima. Its elegant clubhouse had burned to the ground many years ago, and now the greens and fairway lay smothered in sagebrush as the desert reclaimed everything but the original sand traps, and perhaps a few scattered memories.

A low chain-link fence covered with vines separated the east-ern section of our land from a neighbor, whose yard was littered with rusting old tractors and other farm equipment. The residents lived in a small ranch, located about two hundred yards from his odd collection and the fence. Nestled in the center of the yard, sur-rounded by the tractors, sat a two-story wooden building. Its red paint had faded to almost pink, but it still resembled a Midwestern barn. I later learned my friendly neighbors had grown up in the Midwest and that the "barn" provided shelter for tools, tractor pails, and an assortment of other things, which could best be described as junk. The rusting collection was the husband's way of remembering an early life on a farm.

As I drove to our ranch that first morning I attempted to calm Trooper by talking to him softly. I know he gave my monologue attention, for he became quiet. How much he truly understood remains unknown. If I was silent he began to grumble and cry again.

I explained to the cat that we were not going to see Doctor Marg at the pet hospital, which I am sure was what he was expecting (why else would I put him in the crate?). I began to tell him about his new home with lots of trees and places to explore.

As I spoke of our future, my thoughts drifted back to our first house. So many memories must be put aside. That would be difficult because my relationship with the cat began in that house after I brought him home from the cat hospital. I had watched as he recovered from a near-death experience. We grew together as Chi and I raised him as our child.

When young, neither human nor cat can concentrate on a complex thing for long. Both are easily distracted. But somewhere along the way the development is no longer equal. The human outdistances the feline in mentality, but that doesn't mean that the cat stops learning. There are those who believe that the cat's behavior is based strictly on instinct, all activity performed with the absence of learning. Those people don't know cats.

Of course, cats depend on instinct in their complex pattern of behavior. For instinct, an animal needs no training or teaching. But cats often exercise judgment, make decisions, or contemplate situations, and even create games involving imaginary prey, stalking and attacking invisible creatures.

That may be instinct, but after studying cats, especially my domesticated wild cat, I have concluded there must be a wonderful combination of instinct and creative intelligence.

Added to this is the trait called "copycat." As I've learned, that term didn't come about by accident. One cat simply copies or imitates the actions of another, or that of his human friend. Once

Trooper watched me climb an aluminum stepladder to change a light bulb in a ceiling fan. Of course he had no idea why I was changing the bulb, but the climbing part must have looked like fun. Within a few seconds after my descent, the cat climbed up the ladder, one step at a time, smelled the replacement bulb, turned around and descended, face first, using each step. That was a great copy, only I didn't descend face first.

A week before our move I noticed Trooper dashing about the backyard, darting between trees and bushes at full speed. I assumed he was exercising, but it turned out to be a warm up for another game he created. He suddenly stopped and walked slowly towards the concrete block wall that ran along the back of our property. A section of the wall reached a height of six feet, but another section was, for reasons known only to the builder, about ten feet high.

I had watched Trooper hit the top of the six-foot section in an effortless jump, but the ten-foot area might have been out of reach. Of course, he knew he could jump to the top of the six-foot wall and then hop up on the ten-foot section. That process did not present much of a challenge. But he had an experiment in mind. He studied the wall carefully, his head moving as if calculating the feasibility of his plan. Then, suddenly, he turned and ran directly at a redwood patio chair that sat several feet from the wall. He jumped, sprang off the chair, and sailed to the top of the higher wall; a beautiful, exciting sight, perhaps not a major accomplishment for a young wild cat. He strutted along the top, proud that his plan worked so perfectly. Instinct? No doubt, but he thought through a process and then tested it with success.

A week before the wall-jumping project, I prepared to feed the goldfish in our artificial pond. For this, I had a handful of crouton-sized bread pieces in a bowl. As usual, Trooper watched me scatter the bread on the water, the surface breaking with splashes as the fish devoured their meal. The fish were a continual fascination for the cat, who often ran along the water's edge and smacked at the surface with his paw to watch them scoot about. I believe he still had no idea that he could turn the fish into a meal. Perhaps they were more important as a source of amusement.

On that day, I placed the bowl, half full of bread, in the shade next to the sliding glass door and went into the kitchen to join my wife for lunch.

"Look!" Chi said softly as I sat down. "That cat of yours is eating the fish bread!"

I knew he wasn't eating the bread. Bread had no interesting smell or taste to the cat. But I watched as he filled his mouth with the croutons, then strolled to the water and dropped the bread. He sat down and, with ears pointing forward, watched the exciting show as the fish rushed to feed. A copycat, this time with a purpose.

As we prepared to move, I packed all of Trooper's toys in a box, with another box for "Trooper's Treasures," the assortment of things he found in the neighborhood and brought to the house. I planned to have all of this near when I opened his crate at the new home.

To ensure he did not scamper off when the movers arrived with the heavy furniture, I enlisted the aid of Herman, a German emigrant I had recently hired as our resident handyman, to temporarily close a large "cat door" in the wall of the living room. It was a perfect opening for the cat, located next to the fireplace. The former owner used it to push firewood in from the outside. This opening sat about three feet above a concrete walkway. At this cat entrance, Herman erected a small platform to serve as a porch where Trooper could sit and study the yard before beginning a day of exploring.

As I drove up to the front porch and turned off the engine, Trooper grew very quiet. Once inside, I opened the crate and he jumped out.

"Look, Trooper," I said as I opened the box of toys. He showed no interest. Instead, with eyes wide, he turned his head to survey his new environment.

"OK, let's go check out the kitchen."

He followed me closely as we entered the kitchen. As planned, my wife had placed his dry food and water bowl there earlier.

Trooper paused to lap up a small amount of water, and then he was ready to explore the entire house.

As the furniture arrived he began another investigation and spent a few moments smelling each piece. He seemed pleased—that is, not nervous—as he recognized everything.

After the movers departed, I thought it time to allow him to explore his new five-acre domain. I remained with him for the introduction, and we walked slowly side by side. I pointed out the opening in the heavy screen door to the kitchen and lifted him to the porch-like platform at the living room wall so he could see the entrance.

This inspection was thorough and required considerable time. Anyone who has walked with a cat knows that their pace is usually slow, as each thing encountered must pass the smell test. Therefore, our first inspection did not include Herman's guesthouse or the attached office. I planned to save that, knowing he would, no doubt, discover and explore those areas sometime during the night without me.

"I'm going to the house and help unpack," I said.

He paused, looked at me, and then turned to look at the house. Trooper understood part of what I said. I left the front double doors open so he had, for a while, three ways of entering (counting the two cat doors). A few minutes passed and we heard the familiar *crunch-crunch* sound coming from the kitchen. Trooper had entered through the kitchen door to enjoy his lunch.

Almost at once he realized and accepted the fact that he had a new home. Everything he remembered and loved was there, the furniture, complete with his scratch marks, Johnson and ma-ma (Chi), Yellow Bear, fuzzy rats, rope, and his food. Even the goldfish were on site, swimming in a large fountain pool in the front yard. And, most exciting, a large area with trees to climb, bushes and flowers to examine, and so many strange new smells to enjoy.

He quickly lost interest in his toys and in a few days the goldfish received only minor attention. There was simply too much to do in that big new world.

The new home provided him all the domestic comforts he had become accustomed to, while at the same time offering the freedom to be as wild, or "run free," as he desired. The desert for exploration was all around us. But, first, he had to know every inch of his home. This would include meeting and approving of Herman.

Herman was brought to us by friends who assured us that the man was an honest, excellent builder who also knew how to repair almost anything. Herman was recently divorced (we were told that his wife had run off with an Elvis impersonator who was performing in Las Vegas) and needed a job and a place to live. We needed a builder and repairman, so I made Herman an offer. If he remodeled the building for office space, a meeting room, and a small warehouse, he could live in the attached guest house, rent free, as long as we owned the ranch. He could decorate his living quarters to fit his needs. A property as large as ours, with home and the other buildings, would need constant attention, and my work with the gift shop left little time to devote to maintaining the property. Therefore, Herman would have a job working for us after all the remodeling was complete. He accepted my offer. Herman's thick German accent occasionally resulted in miscommunication and my college German didn't really do much to help the situation. But he was, indeed, a master builder and understood my repair and construction needs, often working late into the evening with typical German efficiency to complete different phases of the project. His first assignment, the remodeling of the guesthouse, would be the most important, as he would live there. The finished product was nothing short of magnificent. The kitchen was equipped with all modern appliances and the bathroom included a shower with tub and a beautiful tile floor, all installed by Herman.

Herman's personal appearance, however, was in complete contrast to his work ethics, and his personality would best be described as a bit odd. His brown hair, streaked with gray, was constantly unkempt. We never saw him freshly shaved, and there was always a three- or four-day growth of gray-black whiskers, which matched his eyes. His seldom smiles revealed a few teeth missing.

Though he was not a big man, he was equipped with powerful arms and hands suited to his occupation. We had been assured by the people who introduced him to us that he could "repair or build most anything," and that, he could.

But there were mysteries about the man. We never knew his age, for example. Anytime we inquired we received a different answer, always within a few years of the last answer. He related an endless number of stories of his past, yet remained very vague on just how he arrived in Las Vegas. We assumed he followed his wife, for she, like her new husband, was an "entertainer," or so he once said.

As to his prior profession, we were given different stories over a period of time. For example, he had been a Formula One race car driver for an unnamed German auto manufacturer, though we learned he knew little about automobiles, except how to drive one. He said he once owned a large nightclub, where beautiful women arrived from Russia and Poland, begging for a job, and would do "anything to get one"; we didn't inquire further into what that would entail.

Herman also claimed to be a master chef of European cuisine, who had performed his art on German television, viewed by millions. And then there was the time when he became dean of a "beauty school" and a professional photographer for leading glamour magazines.

We gave little credence to the stories, but they were amusing, especially during slow times at the office.

Most important, though, he was respectful to Chi and myself and attempted to befriend Trooper, who followed him about from time to time, but at a safe distance. There seemed to be an element of caution for both cat and repairman. The cat appeared concerned with the fact that Herman often carried a tool in his hand, a hammer or saw. Observing what the tool could do caused that concern. But, when "unarmed," the cat often approached the man.

We never were able to convince Herman that the cat was tame. He once said to me, "That cat could kill a big animal if he wanted to. I've seen his long teeth. He is *Jaeger* (hunter), he is!"

So, with mutual respect, the two got along, although Trooper kept a careful eye on Herman. The man actually admired the cat, and believed he should always report Trooper's location as the cat explored the property. And, thanks to Herman, the work at our ranch was completed on or ahead of schedule.

It was a good thing that all the ranch projects were moving according to my plans, for our life would be changing in an unexpected way.

We received disturbing news from the hotel management where we had operated our gift shop for several years. As is so often the case with casino-hotel resorts in Las Vegas, this one planned a major renovation. Our gift shop area, we were told, would become part of a new, "vastly expanded buffet." We must make plans to close the shop within two years, an exact date to be issued later.

We depended on the profit from the shop for our survival, and now must create a new business that would replace the income we were about to lose.

Chiaki had a Japanese friend who was employed by another hotel as their international marketing manager. He made an interesting suggestion as to an alternative. I had driven this man and three of his contacts, executives for a Japanese airline, on an off-road desert trail ride in my H1 Hummer. They were thrilled with the short introduction to the desert. All of the riders encouraged the same idea—that I should start an off-road, scenic desert tour business. At the time, Japanese tourists were flooding into Las Vegas, and most had never seen a Hummer except on television news.

Chi and I began to explore different trails in the area and selected a few we believed would be idea for a brief education on our desert.

Ninety percent of Nevada is owned by the US Federal Government under the protection of the Department of the Interior, and most of that percentage is controlled by the Bureau of Land Management (BLM). Anyone may use trails approved by the BLM, but if one is operating commercially, then a "special use permit" is required. BLM attempts to ensure that drivers keep their speed under twenty-five miles per hour (a good idea if one wants to still have his vehicle together at the end of the drive) and remain on existing, approved trails. That is, one should not drive off a trail and into the desert. That action would destroy plants and the fragile desert "crust," a three- or four-inch layer of organic matter that protects the earth from erosion while providing a base for plant seeds to survive.

With our necessary BLM permits, we still needed a county and state business license, as well as a Nevada Transportation Authority certificate. Once we had all of these in hand, plus our commercial insurance (required by all agencies), we were ready to start our desert tours. At last we were ready to show the public the Mojave.

We would be conducting our tours through the beautiful Red Rock Canyon Conservation area with its 200,000 acres of spectacular limestone and red Aztec sandstone cliffs. Some were thousands of feet in elevation. Here, Chi and I pointed out as many interesting points as possible during a three-hour visit into the area. The exciting phase of the tour was when we actually drove "off-road" on BLM trails so people could see the desert from "the inside out." I believed this phase to be important because other tour companies only drove around the desert on blacktop roads and did not enter as we did. We began our tours with a Hummer H1, the original Hummer very similar to the famous Humvee. This was a perfect vehicle, powerful and safe, in which to carry our passengers on the off-road trails. Also, it gave us a great marketing tool as, at the time, most had only seen the vehicle during TV news coverage of the Gulf War.

In this canyon a photographer has a natural landscape paradise. Besides fantastic stone formations, thickets of Joshua trees appear to guard the valley with the Spring Mountains in the background.

The majestic Joshua, often hundreds of years in age, are really not trees, but members of the lily family. They were named by a group of Mormon pioneers as they crossed the Mojave Desert on their way to Utah. The large plant's unique shape reminded them of the Biblical Joshua, reaching his hands to the sky in prayer. The Joshua tree name has held since the mid-1840s.

The Old Spanish Trail passes through the Conservation area. Travelers frequently camp at the oasis now known as Blue Diamond, so named by early prospectors who claimed that water in the desert "is as rare as a blue diamond."

Once off road, the passengers were told to stay alert for animals like the protected desert tortoise, kit fox, coyote, and bobcat. Except for the tortoise, however, these are mostly seen after dark. During daylight hours, though, we expected to see the elegant red-tailed hawk and ravens. Large animals such as the mountain lion, mule deer, and bighorn sheep are found at higher elevations and likely would not be visible. But there are always a great variety of plants, lizards, and snakes to discuss and photograph.

Every day on the trail I thought about Trooper when the name bobcat came up. I believed I was needed at the ranch to watch over him during his early years. The solution to my concern was simply to hire a driver, train him, and maintain contact by two-way radio. Chi prepared to educate young Japanese women to be narrators for the Japanese tourists. The business soon grew to the point where we needed to purchase two additional Hummers and hire drivers as we expanded our contacts to customers from a great variety of countries.

There was yet another phase to be added to our tour option list—mining towns, or ghost towns.

The Old Spanish Trail, which passed through the Las Vegas oasis, attracted Mormon missionaries in 1855. They farmed the land and erected an adobe fort, but evacuated the area to return to Utah at the beginning of the Utah or Mormon War in 1857. After the Civil War a number of ranchers settled at the oasis, but soon a railroad was constructed linking Los Angeles and Salt Lake City.

The steam engines required water, and so did the workers. The Las Vegas oasis had all the water they needed.

Las Vegas became a city around 1909, thanks in part to the railroad, and was home to several hundred people. By 1930 the population reached 5,000.

But before Las Vegas the city was born, there were numerous towns with populations of 1,000 to 5,000 people scattered about Nevada. These were the mining communities, founded because someone struck precious metals, either gold or silver. They, too, needed water to survive, and if either the ore or water (often both) ran out, so did the people. Many of the towns were deserted long before Las Vegas became a city, and the miners, prospectors, and business people moved on to the next boom town. The abandoned town became a ghost town.

Two ghost towns were located within an hour of Las Vegas and our ranch. They were added to our list of tours. With fully qualified new drivers, I could once again spend time with my friend, the cat.

CHAPTER 9
New Territory, New Friends

"If you tame me, we shall need each other."

Antoine de Saint-Exupéry, *The Little Prince*

I REMAINED AS EXCITED AS Trooper while we explored our new property. I knew the cat had been busy at night investigating the area, yet he came to my bed before dawn and snuggled next to me by pushing my arm aside to form a comfortable pocket.

When I strolled about the land, the cat was always nearby, often only a few yards away, darting between bushes. He behaved as if he were my "wing man," protecting my flank. Trooper knew the land belonged to him and assumed the responsibility of guarding me.

Indeed, it was a comfort having him near during those walks. I knew nothing could slip up on him for the cat always appeared in alert mode.

After a walk I went to our office building and settled down to read through the daily paperwork necessary for our business.

Herman had already cut a hole in the office door through which the cat could pass when he pleased. He usually entered after his morning territory check and jumped to the corner of our eight-foot desk to take a nap. He showed no interest in the ringing phone or the sound of shuffling papers.

Across from me sat my office manager, Teri, a thirty-two-year-old attractive blonde with a phone voice that melted even the coldest solicitor. Her duties included the screening of incoming phone calls, placing most of the orders for our gift shop, paying bills, and processing payroll. In addition, she was a master on the computer, a talent I have never equaled. But most impressive was her pleasant personality and her ability to interact with a variety of characters. If I sound prejudiced, I am. Teri is my daughter.

Teri, her twin brother Mike, and her younger sister Nora were raised in Phoenix by their mother after our divorce, while I stayed behind in Chicago. My children came to visit from time to time or I journeyed to Arizona to be with them. Many years later, when the children were young adults, I married Chiaki and within a year Teri and her husband moved to Las Vegas to take advantage of a lucrative job market. Teri's husband was in the home construction business and Teri went to work for a bank. But soon Teri gave birth to my first grandchild, Taylor, a girl. After that she had two more girls, Megan and Jordan, each about two years apart in age. She resigned her position at a local bank to be a full-time mother. Fortunately, she had a friendly neighbor who became their babysitter, meaning that Teri was free to go to work for me as my part-time personal secretary.

I often recall one of Teri's visits to our home shortly before we relocated to the ranch. It was two months after the birth of her first child. Trooper had been sleeping somewhere in the yard that morning, and hearing our conversation, he decided to come into the house for a visit. The cat, then still a youngster, strolled into the living room where we were all seated. Suddenly he stopped and lowered his body almost to the carpet, assuming an alert position. The hair on his back bristled and his nose twitched rapidly. He was shocked by the sight of a pale, hairless animal on the living room floor. It was a creature he had never seen before. This strange animal appeared trapped in some kind of chair. Its legs were moving about and it was making peculiar sounds. *What animal is this,* the cat must have thought. *Is it dangerous? Is it here to take my food? I will carefully investigate.*

Trooper found Teri's two-month-old daughter to be an interesting discovery. Trooper had seen larger children before and learned, like most cats, to avoid them. Children can pull tails, jerk fur, and even throw things at cats. To the cat, this creature appeared harmless, but he had to be sure of that before letting it preside in peace. Trooper moved slowly forward, closing the distance to the baby. We watched with some concern as the cat began to circle the child, moving closer with each pass.

"Look at him," Teri said with serious concern. "What is he doing?"

I knew Trooper would not harm the baby. "He's testing to see how far baby can jump. He has no idea what she is or what she can do. He just wants to be sure it is harmless," I answered assuredly.

Trooper paused about three feet from the child, then turned and started towards the kitchen. He stopped midway and turned to stare back at the baby for a minute. And after a short staring contest, his first meeting with a human infant had ended peacefully. He encountered Teri's other babies with only mild interest— they were harmless and boring. And from there, Trooper and Teri formed a friendship that day, an important occasion because we all would soon share the same desk.

A few days after arriving at the ranch we received a guest, Mr. Jim Butler, our neighbor from across the road. This tall, gray-haired gentleman with a ruddy complexion arrived in an electric-powered golf cart, explaining that the few hundred yards separating our homes was too far for an "old fellow" to walk.

Jim was eighty years old and a retired Navy man, having served almost thirty years. He and a "Navy buddy" left the military the same year and together moved to Las Vegas. This buddy came to visit him each week and they discussed how happy they were to be in the dry climate of the Mojave Desert.

"I had too many years of humidity and mosquitoes in the South Pacific," Jim said. "Here, we don't have either, and I like that!"

With a laugh, Jim stated that he was the "self-appointed area historian." His wealth of local knowledge, which he subsequently relayed to Teri and me, substantiated that claim. He had settled on a ranch about twenty years prior, and could remember when Prima's golf course was abandoned. He recalled that the country clubhouse burned to the ground in a fire set by vandals, and that the manager's home soon met the same fate. All that remained there were a few pine trees near a stone foundation. The golf course, grown over with sagebrush and creosote bushes, had become unrecognizable as a once active playground.

"That's a good looking bobcat you got there!" Jim exclaimed. "I've heard some make good pets."

"How did you recognize him as a bobcat?" I replied.

"Oh, I knew right away. He's a beauty. I saw plenty bobcats around here in the old days before your place was built and civilization with its automobiles chased them away. A band of coyotes competed with the big cats for natural food . . . rabbits and such . . ."

"Coyotes?"

"Yes sir. About seven of them originally. But that pack began to kill pet dogs and cats, so people fought back . . . shot a few of 'em."

"Some are still out there?"

"Yep. Maybe only four remaining. You'll hear them at night when they come near your place. Your cat could kill one or two, but he don't stand no chance against a pack."

Jim noticed the concerned expression on Teri's face.

"Don't worry, ma'am," he continued. "Your cat may be peaceful, but he's still wild in his soul. You can't change that. If need be, he can fight like hell using them claws and long teeth of his. But, you know, he climbs trees faster than you can snap your fingers. One on one he'll lick any coyote stupid enough to test him. But he's smarter than them coyotes. More than likely he'll scamper up a tree to avoid a fight."

"That's good to know, Mr. Butler," Teri said, casting a quick glance at me.

"Them coyotes are the serial killers around here! Always have been, but it won't be long until folks kill 'em off. I know they must hunt for food but this pack has started killing for the fun of it . . . not even eating all their kills.

"Well," I chimed in, "I never liked killers of any kind. Let's hope they decide to move to a deeper part of the desert."

"Not likely," said Jim Butler. Then he added that he was always available to help us, if we needed him. As he started to climb into his cart he stated, "Civilization is moving in on us, you know. I heard that the old golf course is gonna be leveled. Developers plan to build medium-priced homes on the east side of the road and elegant ones on the west."

He shook his head and added, with an element of sadness to his voice, "That will bring more traffic on this old road. Guess I'll be needing something faster than a golf cart to come over to see ya. I hope that beautiful cat of yours don't turn wild and leave you. I'd like to see him again."

Butler turned the key, which resulted in the cart's motor eliciting a high-pitched, electrical shirring sound.

With Jim's departure, Teri and I returned to our work at the desk, but in a few minutes were interrupted by another guest, this time an unwanted one.

Trooper, who had been asleep near my left arm, suddenly awoke. He sat up, ears pointed towards the open doors, his eyes fixed on something we at first didn't see. Then, in a crouched position, he moved slowly to the desk's edge.

My eyes searched the room. There was our intruder only a few feet away, running towards us. It was a large, opaque scorpion, his tail cocked up, stinger poised for a victim.

"Teri! Look!" I shouted, pointing towards the scorpion. But as the words left my lips, Trooper sprang forward, landing a few inches from the arthropod. The next movement came so fast I could not determine what he actually did. We heard the *crunch*. Trooper had eaten the scorpion, leaving only the tail with its stinger on the floor. He leaped gracefully to our desk, curled up, and appeared to fall asleep.

"Gosh, Dad!" Teri exclaimed. "Did he get stung?"

"Don't know. He doesn't act like anything hurts. Try to get Doctor Marg on the phone. Let's find out if we need to take him to the hospital."

Teri placed the call and handed me the phone. I heard the doctor's voice and explained.

"I know the sting from that kind of scorpion can make humans very sick, but it's not deadly. What about cats?"

She responded quickly, "If Trooper is not licking or chewing at a wound then he didn't get stung. But if he did . . . or in the future if he does, get him over here. We can treat him."

"I think he is OK. Just wanted to be sure." I said. But then inquiringly added, "How did he avoid getting stung?"

"Instinct and speed," she answered, as if it were the simplest thing the world. "He knows he must avoid the stinger and speed, in this case, is his best weapon. He's simply faster than the scorpion, killing it with a fatal bite before the stinger can strike."

"Really?"

"House cats in this area often kill scorpions, but they seldom eat them. Remember, Trooper has natural instincts ingrained into his very DNA. People in some parts of China eat scorpions, so your cat's diet isn't strange. There is only one dangerous scorpion around Las Vegas. It's called the Arizona Bark Scorpion. They arrive on the leaves of imported palm trees, and are darker in color, usually brown."

I thanked Doctor Marg and related the conversation to Teri, whose response was simply, "Ugh!"

In the years to come, Trooper's war with scorpions continued. We found pieces of their tail sections from time to time on the porch and driveway. He seemed determined to eradicate the species. Scorpions have been on earth for over a hundred million years, but their survival in our area seemed questionable.

There was one small creature, however, that he both hated and feared. A large, noisy blackbird flew, ran, and hopped about parking lots in town and residential neighborhoods, creating quite a racket with its ear-piercing shriek. I soon learned this bird, with long black tail feathers, is called a great-tailed grackle.

All cats in the valley hate grackles, for the bird knows that felines can climb trees and threaten their nests. To frighten off potential enemies (including dogs and people), grackles dive and peck at the heads of their intruders.

At first, Trooper did not use his ability to defend himself—rather he would seek the cover of bushes and other places the bird could not easily reach. Using his speed, the cat could knock the grackle to the ground with one swing of his paw. The cat was exercising restraint and had, I guessed, no desire to harm the bird.

But the day finally came when Trooper could take no more of annoying attacks and decided to strike back. As usual, the grackle began his diving attack while the cat strolled towards our office from the front porch. Catching the cat in the open area provided the best opportunity for the bird. This time the cat decided to turn quickly and spring into the air. At four feet above the ground he slapped the bird with a paw.

The grackle tumbled along the pavement, jumped up, hopped a few feet, and took flight, landing on a tree limb, apparently unhurt.

Trooper chose not to pursue his enemy, but continued his journey to the office. Had our bobcat become compassionate, or did he know that grackles don't taste good? Either way, the grackle had learned a lesson and never tried to attack the cat again.

Over the next two years Trooper remained busy exploring his territory as if it were brand-new. He napped on my desk part of the day, and no matter how occupied with adventures, he slept in my bed most every night.

I had given all nearby residents a photo and description of my cat when we first moved into the area so they would not mistake him for a true "wild" cat. Naturally they were concerned for the safety of their own pets, but I assured them they had nothing to fear from Trooper. He avoided dogs of all sizes. One yap or bark and he was out of there. During the many years we lived at our ranch there was never one report of Trooper harming a pet. The main concern was coyotes. Everyone feared them and attempted to guard their pets from those predators.

One April morning I heard Herman calling me with his deep voice.

"Trooper has fuzzy animal!" he reported.

"What kind of animal?"

"A little fuzzy animal!"

Trooper moved past me, heading towards the house and presumably his cat door. Indeed, a small animal dangled from his mouth.

This came as no shock. Almost all cats, if given the opportunity, hunt small rodents. Wild cats, for their survival, must be professional at that job.

I returned to the house, prepared to clean a gory mess in one of the rooms before my wife discovered it. To my surprise, Chi met me at the front door.

"We have a zoo in the living room. I was on the way to the office to get your help," she said, with a slight smile.

"A zoo? Did Trooper deposit a dead rat in there just now?"

"Not dead. Not rat. Chipmunk!" she stated, pointing at the living room.

Trooper was racing about the floor, chasing his fuzzy animal. As he did, other chipmunks scampered here and there in desperation to escape their captor.

"I've counted three so far," Chi said, "plus the one he just brought in!"

"Four! All alive?"

"Very much alive," she replied. "I think he wants them alive to play with and has plans to eat them."

I sat down and watched as the small, striped rodents with their pudgy cheeks raced about the floor. They were lively and speedy, their flat, bushy tails with white and brown fur held high, appearing to enjoy the game of hide, catch, and hide again.

Trooper had worked hard to accumulate those playmates and relocate them safely to the house. I doubt, however, if they were as happy as the hunter.

The cat disappeared through his kitty door, but within a few minutes, while I calculated how to remove all his toys, he reappeared carrying another chipmunk, which he released unharmed. This one was reddish-brown in color, and like the others had stripes on the side of his face, extending down the back to the tail.

It's likely that those feisty creatures were not actually chipmunks, but desert white-tailed antelope squirrels. The two are closely related and have a resemblance. Either way, to Trooper they must have appeared as if his little fuzzy toys had come to life, like the characters in the *Nutcracker* ballet.

The chipmunk roundup continued into the next day, and then, as suddenly as it began, it all ended. Trooper lost interest in the hunt and the game he created. None of the little creatures were harmed, but it required two more days for Herman and me to capture and return them all to the wild.

Over the next few years the cat and I played together whenever time permitted. I, of course, am not a cat and never had the ability to pretend to be one. Trooper did not always understand that fact, and often led me into different corners of our property in search of some adventure he had in mind. There were places he wanted us to go together, places such as narrow paths through the underbrush and up the steep bank of our gully. This came easily for him, but was nearly impossible for me.

Seldom did I learn exactly what he wanted me to see, but sometimes the obvious lay before me: the remains of a half-eaten jackrabbit or a pile of feathers from an unknown bird. Those, I assume, were his prize kills. He was proud of his accomplishments, and I, on all fours, felt obligated to praise and thank him for sharing those important secrets.

More than once he led me to a large tree in the front yard for a climbing lesson. First, he dashed up the tree to show me how it should be done. He looked down and made yowling sounds, as what I interpreted as words of encouragement. Once, in response to his request, and pretending to be a cat, I started climbing up, one limb at a time. Trooper left his position and came down to check on my progress. He brushed my cheek with his whiskers to indicate satisfaction. He turned then, climbed higher and paused to give his yowling sounds once more. Apparently my climbing failed to meet with his approval.

My energy soon diminished. Trooper leaned over a large limb, his front legs dangling, and watched me carefully descend. I dropped to the ground with an audible groan. And there I sat so my breathing could return to normal.

The cat joined me, brushing his body against my leg while purring.

"I'm not very good at climbing, am I?" I asked him. "Sorry to disappoint you."

Trooper responded with another brush of my leg. Cats are so forgiving, even if they cannot understand human failure. To him, it must have been confusing to see all the things his human could and could not do. As humans, we build, provide food, drive cars, and on and on. Yet I could not do something like climb a tree with any skill at all.

The cat ascended the tree once more, perhaps to demonstrate the technique, or maybe simply for the fun of it.

As the months sped by, life continued this way for the cat and me. When time from business permitted, we played together, exploring his special places. But of course, most of his life's activities outside remained a mystery. It seemed that as soon as I learned his routine, I would soon discover that he had changed it as if to keep me uncertain of his next destination.

In our home there was one mystery that I never solved to this day: how do cats know the time you wish to wake, or when the alarm clock will sound? But perhaps a more difficult question to answer is, why will the cat wake you minutes before the alarm sounds?

There are many theories on the subject, some centering on the exact purpose of that behavior. None, to me, explain why cats do it.

The bedroom ceiling fan had been installed by our ranch home's original owner long ago. We never used it. The bedroom temperature always remained comfortable, whether it was winter or summer.

Curiosity finally captured me one afternoon. I decided to test the old fan by clicking through its performance at a variety of speeds, controlled by a wall switch near the head of our bed.

I switched it on and off a few times. The giant blades rotated with an odd clanking sound, indicating something was not right with its mechanisms. So I decided to turn it off during its highest rotation speed.

I wasn't the only one watching the fan's rotation. Trooper had entered the room and was sitting at my side. As the blades' rotation slowed, he decided to spring into action. With an easy pounce onto the bed he was in a perfect position to complete his mission.

Before I could grab the cat or shout a command, he leaped onto the fan and succeeded in wrapping his front legs around one blade, about halfway between its end and the motor.

During the next few moments, as the fan continued to rotate, Trooper struggled to get his rear legs up and around the blade; the force of the rotation was too much. He held on. The fan rotated once, twice, three more times, the cat dangling as if he were part of the fixture.

Then, the clanking sound became louder and developed into more of a grinding of metal sound. The fan's rotation suddenly stopped, causing Trooper to lose his grip.

So now my bedroom had a flying cat, at least for a second or two, as Trooper went sailing several feet through the air.

He landed perfectly on all four paws, shook himself, and strolled casually from the room. With a serious wound, the fan now hung from the ceiling at a thirty-degree angle. My guess is that it had already been suffering from a mechanical malfunction. My twenty-eight-pound cat put it out of its mechanical misery.

The cat had seen the fan many times but hadn't known it could move. Observing its rotation for the first time alerted him to a potential danger (at least to the cat) in the room. From that day on, the cat never gave the fan a glance.

But while I stood there contemplating my next move, Chiaki entered and was quick to give a comment on the fan's peculiar position. "Looks no good," she observed. "Herman doesn't like to fix electrical stuff. Maybe you call fan man."

"Fan man just worked on it." I chuckled to myself.

"What?"

"Oh." I spoke clearly. "I think a fan man will try to sell us a new one. We never used the fan anyway."

CHAPTER 10

Disappearing

"What sort of philosophers are we who know nothing or the origin or destiny of cats."

Henry David Thoreau

A NYONE WHO HAS FACED M AJOR surgery knows the multitude of worries that follow the doctor's announcement. I had to have colon surgery as soon as possible. It seemed I was more worried about the business continuing successfully and about my cat thriving than I was about my own physical condition. But I was blessed with caring, hardworking people who helped to maintain the family business; Teri managed our office, while Herman and Chi watched over all activities and still found time to visit me each day at the hospital during my three-week absence.

So, with everything under control, I had only to concentrate on my recovery and a remaining worry . . . Trooper.

Understanding my concern for the cat, everyone had a "Trooper story" to relate during phone calls and visits to set my mind at ease while I was away. Teri told of him taking naps on her desk during the day, Herman reported that Trooper continued to patrol the perimeter of our property, and Chi assured me he slept with her each night. But she also told me the cat spent a few minutes going from room to room for the first several days I was away and scratched on closet doors until she opened them to prove I wasn't hiding inside.

Some say that cats are only curious, but not intelligent enough to comprehend why a friend has disappeared. They believe the cat understands whether one is there or not there, and nothing more. That conclusion, I am certain, is incorrect. Based on my years with Trooper and conversations with many domestic cat owners, I can report that cats, like dogs, grieve for a missing friend, human or animal, and they often attempt to learn where that friend has gone. Their logic may be limited to considering places that they remember visiting with their friend, such as a previous home, office, or their animal hospital. It remains a mystery as to just what else their mind may consider.

This worried me. Would Trooper take off on a journey? And therein lay another mystery. How do cats find their way home after wandering for miles? Perhaps only cats know the answer.

My wife's report that Trooper slept with her assured me he had not wandered off—yet, anyway. But then I received the good news. The doctors assured me that all tests for cancer had negative results. I was cancer free and, after those three weeks, was released from the hospital and could go home. I would, however, be restricted to walking no more than a short distance the first three days. But the surgery was successful and I was healing.

Chi prepared the guest bedroom for my recovery. It had a connecting bathroom that required very little walking to reach, perfect for those first few days.

With Chi at the wheel, we entered the circular driveway and drove to the front of the house. My reception committee waited on the front porch. Teri and Herman stood with broad smiles, and next to them sat Trooper. In this time with us thus far, he had learned to recognize the sound of our car, distinguishing it from all others. No doubt he knew I would be arriving because Teri and

Herman were waiting for someone special, and hearing our car gave the final clue.

As Herman helped me from the car, Trooper came and brushed against me. I spoke to him while scratching the top of his head, then he disappeared into the house.

I hobbled to the guest room with Chi supporting me on one side. There was Trooper, sitting at the end of the bed, his ears pointing forward, his big eyes studying me.

My meal that first night, which Chi delivered on a tray, consisted of soup, ginger ale, mashed potatoes, and Jell-O, all of which were prescribed by the doctor. Trooper believed he must approve the meal, so without hesitation, he leaped onto the bed and smelled each item on the tray. Like me, he was unimpressed. He then inspected my bandages, his face appearing concerned as he apparently recognized the bitter odor of antiseptic from his days in the animal hospital. His mind must have pondered what was wrong with his friend Johnson. Maybe that horrible food had something to do with my problems.

My first night home, I drifted off to sleep with the cat snuggled next to me. Trooper believed his presence and warmth would aid my recovery. I awoke shortly after daybreak, having slept deeply for the first time in many nights. No one woke me for a blood draw or to check my blood pressure. I stretched and let my left arm collapse to my side. And that's when I felt it: my hand had come to rest on something strange, something with . . . feathers!? I sat up slowly. A dove and a pigeon, very dead but still warm, were within easy reach. I knew their purpose at once. I called to my wife.

"Chi! Could you come in here, please?"

She was at my side in an instant.

"What's wrong?" she exclaimed.

"Nothing, really," I answered. "But just to be sure, I've got to ask, did you put these dead birds here?"

"Oh my gosh. No! Of course not! I checked on you about midnight. You were sleeping so soundly. Trooper was gone. There were no birds here then. He must have brought them later. There is no blood on the bed. How did he kill them? Why didn't he eat them outside?"

"I don't know how he killed them," I answered. "Maybe I'll ask him later. These birds are for me. If he wanted them, you're right. He would have eaten them outside. Guess he thinks I need protein. He checked my dinner carefully and found nothing of interest last night."

"What are you going to do?"

"Get me a plastic shopping bag."

She returned with the bag and watched as I removed a few feathers and scattered them about the bed.

"What's that for?" she asked.

"I want him to think I ate the birds," I replied.

"Feathers . . . and, everything?" she joked.

"Sure. He does."

I placed the birds in the bag and tied the top.

"Ask Herman to put this in the big trashcan by the road and close the lid tight. Let's find out what Trooper will do next."

That night I struggled to stay awake, but fell asleep with Trooper at my side. He had spent an initial moment smelling the feathers and I thanked him for the special meal. My mind was still on "hospital time" and I awoke a little after dawn. Trooper was gone. In his place at my side lay my evening meal; another dove and a black lizard, its species unknown to me. Once again I called for Chi to bring a plastic bag.

"Ugh!" she exclaimed with a glance at what Trooper had delivered. "No pigeon this time?"

I laughed. "I guess not. Nothing like variety. I think he is testing to see what I prefer."

"Then, why don't you leave that ugly lizard and see what his reaction will be," she suggested. "I don't think he eats lizards."

"Don't know if he does. I doubt it, but that's a good idea."

The third morning I found a newest selection: a dove and some kind of brown rat, the likes of which, in all my years of desert wanderings, I had never seen before. The lizard had disappeared during the night, carried away by my hunter friend.

So Trooper eventually—or so he believed—learned my preference: doves. I guess the brown rat was just a special treat. No doubt, Trooper believed he had assisted in my recovery by furnishing me fresh meat. He knew I could not provide for myself. I had given him food over the years, now he returned the favor.

This time both the bird and rat went to the trash. Although I'll never know if he believed I actually ate those creatures, he seemed pleased, that I must have enjoyed it all. Other than the lizard, I always "cleaned my plate," so to speak.

The next day I received permission from my doctor to walk about the place and enjoy real food in the kitchen. Trooper watched as I finished a large cheeseburger. Of course I saved a piece for him. The next morning there were no dead birds, no lizard, and no brown rat, only Trooper sleeping next to me.

As weeks went by I gained strength, walked that short distance to the office each day, and began to drive. The bandages were removed and life returned to normal.

One night during my recovery, Trooper did not sleep in my bed, and the next morning we couldn't find him in the house, office, or anywhere else about the property. At first this didn't alarm me. He had ventured off on some special mission and remained absent a day or two before. The morning of the third day he had not returned and I became concerned. That night, near 11 p.m., we heard the unmistakable scream of one bobcat, followed in quick succession by another. Had it come from Trooper?

I was college-aged the first time I heard a bobcat scream. That had been long ago, in 1955 and in the hardwood forest of western Kentucky. The wonderful smell of autumn leaves permeated the countryside, a wilderness filled with oak, maple, dogwood, and hickory, and their brilliant colored leaves that fell like raindrops around us.

My friends and I had followed the owner of that beautiful land, an old farmer, up a path to a limestone shelf, which protruded from the earth like a swollen lower lip. There were Native American carvings in that stone, the farmer told us, and being science students, we wanted to see them.

Suddenly a scream broke through the soft sound of falling leaves. We all stopped and looked for the source. The old farmer laughed at our response. My first thought was that the scream came from a panther. We were in "Panther Valley," had crossed "Panther Creek" a mile back, and were only a few miles from (truly named) Panther, Kentucky. But we had been assured there had been no mountain lions, or panthers as they were once called, in the area for over seventy-five years. Nonetheless, we each heard the scream.

"So ya heard the lady scream, did ya?" the old man said.

"What lady?" my friend inquired.

"The lady of the woods," the farmer replied. "She has been roaming these parts for years. Carries a long knife and tomahawk and hunts for her food with bow and arrow. Makes her bows from Osage wood. Indians knew that's the best for bows."

I believe that my friends and I all chuckled at the same time.

"Go ahead and laugh," the old man mocked, but his response was interrupted by another scream, this one with a shriller sound.

"Yep, that the lady," he added.

"You ever seen this lady?" I asked. I had heard many legends in the backwoods of Kentucky, most involving Native American folk tales, monsters, or strange characters living in the wilds.

"Nope. Not me," he replied. "But my grandfather seen her and his grandfather before."

"She must be very old," I joked.

More guffaws from my friends followed.

"Oh, yes. She's old, but beautiful. She's got raven black hair and green eyes. Runs like a deer and drinks limestone water that smells of sulfur. It's the water what keeps her young. At night, my grandpa said, her eyes flash red like coals."

My eyes continued to scan the woods as the old man entertained my friends with his story.

Then, I saw it. First a blur of brown color, moving silently near the narrow creek about fifty yards away. It was not the beautiful lady of the woods, but instead a large cat. It paused, leaped across the creek, and disappeared between the trees, his color blending with that of the falling leaves. The first bobcat I had ever seen in the wild and I shared only a moment of his life.

But as wonderful as they were, memories like that one were of no comfort to my present concern. With Trooper missing and that late-night scream, coyotes became my greatest worry. We had not heard them howling for several days, and then the sounds were at a great distance. But there was that possibility they had moved closer to our property.

How often pet owners worry for their little friends who have wandered away and did not return when expected. This is nothing new. An 1805 English nursery rhyme states it clearly: Pussy cat, pussy cat, where have you been?

That afternoon, as I worked in my office, my wife's voice came through the two-way radio.

"Come quickly!" she yelled. "I'm in the kitchen. Trooper is here. He's hurt!"

I ran to the house, ignoring the fact that my surgery site had not completely healed. Chi was kneeling next to Trooper as he drank at his water bowl. Blood oozed from wounds in his neck and ear.

"Let's get him to the vet!" I shouted hoarsely as I left to retrieve his hated travel crate. Trooper appeared weak and exhausted and offered no resistance this time as I carefully lowered him in and secured the latches.

Doctor Marg and a female assistant stood by my side in the examination room and opened the top of the crate. As the cat raised his head Doctor Marg lifted him to the stainless steel table.

"Wow" she exclaimed, "you have become such a big boy! You've gained weight since your last visit." Then she added, "Oh, Trooper, Trooper. You gave up another one of your nine lives! So this is number seven now? Could it be number six? How many years have I been patching you up? Six years? I can't remember without looking at your file."

"It's been seven years." I said.

"Seems impossible!"

"You think these wounds were done by a coyote?" I asked.

"No," she replied. "The bite marks are too small for a coyote or dog. He tangled with another cat."

"What kind of cat would be big enough, stupid enough to fight with Trooper?"

"Another bobcat," came the answer.

"Really! Why would they fight? Trooper wouldn't be after a female cat."

"The other cat wouldn't know that," she laughed. "They fight for the same reason domestic cats get into it; most likely, it was over territory. Either Trooper wandered into an area claimed by another cat, or that cat entered his territory. Male wild cats and domestic cats behave the same when it comes to fighting. They resolve the situation in their own way. If they can't settle the disagreement with hissing, growling, and screaming at one another, like humans, they resort to blows and bites."

Doctor Marg turned to me and said, "We got to get this big kitty cleaned up and start an IV with fluids and antibiotics. None of the bites are serious, but our worry is infection. We don't know how much blood he has lost—hopefully, not much. Still, I want to keep an eye on him overnight. Don't worry. He's going to be okay. True to his name, Trooper can survive most anything. Plan to come in about five tomorrow afternoon. I'm going to bandage this ear with the hole in it. I doubt if he'll let it remain in place, though."

"I'll be here at five."

The doctor was silent a moment, then continued, but in a mellow tone.

"We never get used to it, do we? Our pets wander off. We don't know where they are and we make ourselves sick with worry. Our little friends become so much a part of our life. Did you ever stop and think that they worry about us when we are gone longer than they expect? We are the center of their universe. Well, Mr. Johnson, they will always return, if physically capable."

When we arrived home the next evening, Trooper, bandage still in place on his ear, leaped from his crate and went directly to his dry food bowl in the kitchen. The bandage remained on the tip of his ear for about an hour, then it disappeared. We never found it.

CHAPTER 11

The Fox and the Black Cats

"A righteous man has regard for an animal, but the wicked are always cruel."

Proverbs 12:10

IT WAS AFTER 2 A.M. We were later than usual returning home from our hotel gift shop. We had just completed a turn onto our narrow country road from the wide, east-to-west street when something dashed in front of our car, its eyes flashing red in the headlight beams.

"Was that a coyote?" my wife asked.

"No. Too small for a coyote. It stopped over there, under those pine trees next to that old stone foundation."

"Look, a rabbit!" Chi exclaimed, pointing to the foundation.

A large jackrabbit, native to the Southwest, sat peacefully munching on long stems of green grass. Actually a "hare," the jack is much larger than a rabbit and has longer ears, which help regulate body temperature in the desert's scorching heat. Originally called a "jackass rabbit" because of those ears, the creature became famous as a "jackrabbit" after Mark Twain published his 1872 book,

Roughing It. The book recounts Twain's journey with his brother, Orion Clemens, the then Secretary of Nevada Territory, on a journey west. On this trip, Twain became fascinated with the rabbits' ability to elude coyotes. Both predator and prey can reach speeds of over forty miles per hour, but it is the zigzag running style of the rabbit that can keep him from becoming a coyote dinner.

In the Southwest, night was truly a time for animals. Distracted by the large rabbit, we had almost forgotten about the odd little animal that ran in front of our car.

I pulled the car onto the left side of the road and came to a halt. The moon's bright light illuminated the desert floor, giving the appearance of fresh snowfall. But the warm June breeze brought reality and the sweet fragrance of pine needles greeted us as I rolled the window down.

There, bathed in the moonlight, sat the odd little animal, apparently not at all alarmed by our sudden appearance.

"He's cute," Chi observed, "he looks like a toy dog. His ears are so tall!"

The little animal with a black tip on his long, bushy tail waited not far from the front of our car. His gray-and-rust-colored coat appeared glossy in the moonlight and he turned to look at me with large eyes and an alert expression, giving the appearance of a smile on his face. His long nose twitched as he carefully studied us.

"He's a kit fox," I spoke quietly. "A distant cousin of dogs and a closer relative to the red and gray fox in the mountains, only much smaller. Do we have any food in the car?"

"I don't think so. Wait, here's a bag of beef jerky you didn't finish yesterday. Think he'll eat it?"

The fox stood, his eyes locked on me. But the rabbit must have been frightened by our voices, as he stopped eating and became motionless.

"He's sure a little fox." Chi said, "Maybe he's a baby."

"I don't think so. Seems to be full grown. He'll never be larger than a house cat. I don't mean Trooper; an ordinary cat at about six to eight pounds."

I opened the bag of beef jerky and moved slowly towards the grassy area. The jackrabbit gave me a long, uncertain look; then, with casual hops, it disappeared into the darkness. I, not the fox, seemed to have prompted his concern. The fox was smaller and posed no serious threat to the full-grown jack; I, on the other hand, appeared gigantic in comparison.

I placed the strips of jerky on the ground about five feet before me, sat down, and waited to see how he reacted. Would he come to me and take the jerky? With an elegant trot, resembling that of a five-gaited horse, the fox traveled around the car, stopping to sniff in a few places, then stood on his hind legs below the passenger window. His keen sense of smell told him someone was in the vehicle and he stretched, unsuccessfully trying to look inside. He dropped to the ground and trotted in my direction, paused, then began to move in circles around me, coming closer with each pass.

No doubt the fox had seen cars and people before, but never up close. He slowed to a walk, his bushy tail held straight, parallel to the ground, then came to a stop directly in front of me.

I spoke to the fox in a whisper, telling him how beautiful he was and that I had brought him food. I pushed the jerky in his direction and held out both hands, palms pointing upward.

He came to the jerky, sniffed each strip, snatched one, and trotted into the night. I heard a noise behind me and turned. Chi was leaning out the car window with her camera.

"I didn't use the flash," she said. "I thought it might frighten him. Hope the photo comes out. See how he runs! Maybe that's where the dance name came from."

"What dance?"

"The fox trot," she replied with a giggle.

"Funny girl. Look! Here he comes again!"

The fox approached the jerky, sat down, and tilted his head back, startling me with a sharp *yap*. Somewhere in the darkness there followed a *yap* response, and another fox, much smaller than the first, joined us.

In a few moments all the jerky was gone, relocated to a place of safety.

"What an experience," I remarked as I entered the car. "I think the larger fox called the other one once he felt things were safe."

"Where do they find water?" Chi asked as we drove that lonely road a mile to our home. Our wildlife encounter had left her feeling curious.

"The kit fox doesn't need to drink water like other mammals. God put him in this arid environment and gave him the ability to survive on very little water. He gets all the moisture he needs from what he eats."

"So what does he eat, besides beef jerky?" Chi asked jokingly.

"A variety of small creatures, like mice and bugs and little nesting birds. He's a night hunter, but I've seen them playing in the desert during the day."

A few nights later we saw the fox again in the same grassy area. This time we had some leftover baked chicken from our evening meal at the hotel's restaurant. Carrying the plastic to-go box, I walked to the now designated feeding area. The fox smelled the chicken the moment we arrived and came directly towards me, followed closely by the smaller fox. The chicken quickly disappeared.

The fox feeding became routine, mostly with leftovers from the hotel meal. We discovered the little animals had some "table manners." One fox always waited for the other to arrive before eating. Often we watched as they gracefully leaped over sage, like a deer, then returned to that familiar trot as they neared.

Wildlife enthusiasts and government officials discourage the feeding of wild animals such as the kit fox for two reasons. First, they believe that human food is not healthy for wild animals and in many instances, they are correct. Much of the food we eat is not good for us, either. But the kit fox, like the coyote, is a scavenger. His diet is quite diversified: small rodents, garbage, insects, and even a carcass, if it comes to that. Its stomach is designed to digest a plethora of items.

The second reason has more merit. Wildlife enthusiasts, especially those belonging to certain organizations such PETA, BLM, and state and federal wildlife agencies, worry that wild animals may become dependent on food given to them by people and forget how to hunt for survival. Unless the animal has been held in captivity for a long time, I doubt that it will lose the instinct for hunting.

Trooper is an example of this. Raised from a kitten on commercial cat food (and yes, some human food as well), he never lost his hunting instinct. Once we moved to the ranch, until he was too old to hunt, he continued to stalk rabbits, birds, lizards; except for the lizards, he ate what he killed.

Right or wrong, we fed the foxes once or twice a week for almost three months.

The desert, at the edge of town, is quiet late at night and the foxes quickly learned the sound of our car engine. When the car came to a stop they would appear near the side of the vehicle to learn what special treat Chi and I had brought.

One night, as my headlights revealed the foxes waiting at the usual spot, I felt a little guilty. We had no food for them. After a brief discussion, I turned the car around and drove to the nearest all night convenience store. There I purchased a package of hot dogs and returned to feed my waiting friends.

I placed the hot dogs in a row as I had with strips of beef jerky months earlier. The larger fox came forward and sniffed the food, then gave me a curious look as if to ask, *What's this? Where is the good stuff you usually bring?*

After a few moments, the fox carried a hot dog into the darkness. I was in for a surprise. He returned with a twelve-inch stick in his mouth and placed it on the ground in front of me.

How do I respond? He wouldn't understand a game of "fetch" if I tossed the twig, and furthermore, I feared that might frighten him. So, uncertain of his intentions or desire, I picked up the stick and held it next to my cheek, then pressed it to my forehead. I have no idea why I did that. I got up and handed the stick through the open window.

"Keep this for me," I said.

"I got a picture of you, the fox, and the wood. What is he trying to tell you?"

"I wish I knew," I confessed. "He's communicating, but what?"

"Maybe he thinks the hot dog tastes like wood," she replied with a grin.

Nonetheless, the pair ate all the hot dogs, but the purpose of the stick, a special gift, is anyone's guess.

A few days later we returned with some leftover fried chicken. This, I knew, the fox would eat without question. Very few animals can resist the tempting smell of fried chicken. We were in for another surprise.

The fox was waiting, but he had been joined by two black cats. Neither appeared concerned with the other, so I joined the group with the chicken. The cats, one very small with long hair, resembled a Persian; the other, shorthaired, had a white mark on her chest like a marquise diamond. They waited patiently for the foxes to carry off some chicken and then quickly ate the remaining pieces.

I reached to pet the cats, but they backed away.

"Where did they come from?" Chi inquired.

"Don't know," I replied. "They are both females. The closest home is almost a mile past ours. Someone must have dropped them off. Someone who no longer wanted them."

"Dropped them off? That's horrible! How could someone be so cruel to just desert them way out here in the middle of nowhere?"

"People sometimes do horrible things to animals. The cat learns to depend on someone, exchanges lots of love and affection for food and shelter, only to be tossed out like garbage. I doubt if they'll ever trust humans again. I worry that these cats will hang around here, expecting their humans to return someday. They'll starve or coyotes will get them."

"Could we take them home?"

"I don't think I can catch them. Even if I did, how will Trooper behave towards them?"

"How about the animal-rescue people?"

"We could call them, but by the time they get around to this area it will be too late."

"Then what can we do?"

"Well, we can bring food and water tomorrow, and try to come up with a plan."

Walking away from the cats, I felt good about what we were doing. At least we could keep the girls well fed until we had a solution. These were not "outside" cats, judging from the condition of their coats. At least, at one time, they had been well cared for. But even if we fed them, there was still the worry of coyotes.

The kit fox, on the other hand, had little to fear from the coyote. The fox's speed closely matched that of the coyote, and like the jackrabbit, its ability to run and bound over bushes using a zigzag fashion quickly tired the larger predator. Perhaps because of those qualities, coyotes seldom pursue a fox.

I found it interesting that during those nights of feeding, the fox and cats never bothered one another. I fed them a few yards apart and they indicated no interest in the others' food.

A week into feeding the cats, events began to unfold in that section of the desert which, at first, concerned me for the survival of the animals. But in the long run, it provided a solution to the problem. One night during this week, I noticed a few wooden stakes with ribbons attached at the top near the road's edge. I knew, at once, that the area was being surveyed. I passed the feeding area the following afternoon and my heart sank. A large manufactured home on wheels sat only twenty yards from the grove of pine trees. One man with blueprints rolled and held tightly under his arm stood near the creatures' home, talking to another who was wearing a yellow construction helmet.

I stopped my car and walked directly towards the men.

"Hi!" I said. "Sorry to interrupt you fellows. I live about a mile down this road. I'm curious. You getting ready to build something here?"

The men were friendly and gave me a brief description of their company's plans for the old golf course. They had been discussing preparations to level the area for a major real estate development, just as my neighbor, Jim, predicted the year before.

"When is all this work to begin?" I inquired.

"Equipment should arrive tomorrow," he said, "and work will begin a day later."

I wished them good luck and departed.

I don't remember driving that last mile home. I was locked in deep thought about fate of the cats and the little foxes. Would they be crushed in their dens by heavy earth-moving equipment?

That night we stopped to feed the animals as usual. The foxes were there, but no cats. I shone my flashlight beam into the pine trees in hopes they might be hiding there. No cats.

Lights inside the construction cabin for the manufactured home came on, and a man, dressed in gray overalls, appeared in the doorway.

"What are you doing here?" the man shouted as he started towards me.

"I live down this road," I replied. "I've lost two black cats! Have you seen them?"

"Cats? No. I'm the night watchman for this project. I ain't seen no cats. Sorry."

I thanked him, apologized for disturbing his rest, and returned to the car.

"The black cats are gone, aren't they?" Chi asked.

"We'll try again tomorrow night. Maybe they're hiding. I left food for them."

The next night a large bulldozer sat a short distance from the cabin. The equipment had sliced a wide path through the desert, ripping up sagebrush and mesquite along the way. Now they were silent monsters in the moonlight, waiting for the sun to continue their destruction.

The fox did not come to eat. Neither did the cats. The food I left the night before was untouched. We waited, without speaking, for a little over an hour. Then Chi began to cry.

"They're never coming back!" she sniffled. "This construction work frightened them."

"Yes," I said softly.

"But . . . there is no water out there. They will die with no water!"

"The fox will be OK," I said. "They'll find a new place to hunt. They don't need water."

"But the black cats need water! Do they have any chance at all?"

I handed her a Kleenex. I could not bring myself to answer.

"We tried," I said.

CHAPTER 12

The Fox Knows

"The cat has absolute emotional honesty. Human beings may hide their feelings, a cat does not."

Ernest Hemingway

FOR ME, THE BEST CURE for melancholy is to get busy and bury myself in work. But sadness over the apparent loss of the two black cats sunk my wife into depression that proved hard to shake. *Maybe,* I thought, *the solution to that problem would come once the day's work unfolded at the office.*

Teri greeted me with something strange the moment I entered the office.

"Good morning, Dad. Before you get started on anything, you have to know what Trooper is up to."

"What?"

"Herman says that . . . Trooper has cats cornered in the big culvert pipe. The one which goes under the road."

At first the announcement didn't sound like anything important. Then I remembered we had had no cat visitors since our move to the ranch.

"He didn't attack them, did he?"

"No," she replied. "Herman says he's just sitting there, keeping them from coming out of the pipe. He is not in the gully. He's looking down on them from the edge above."

A thought flashed through my mind. I must admit, this was an element of hope for an impossibility.

"Did Herman say what color those cats are?"

"He said there are two cats, both black. Why?" She glanced with a puzzled look, having not really expected me to show this much interest.

I started to the door, turned, and gave an order.

"Call Chi. Tell her to meet me at that spot, where the culvert goes under the road. Tell her to bring a can of wet cat food, one of those Trooper doesn't like."

"You gonna feed those cats?"

"I think I know the cats," I responded with a big smile.

"Herman says they are small. Don't let Trooper hurt them, okay Dad?"

"Don't worry, I won't."

On the way out the door I met Herman returning to the office.

"Trooper still have those cats cornered?"

"Yep. He was there a few moments ago."

"He fighting with them?"

"Not at all! They were just looking at each other. No sound. Like they're thinking about something. Trooper on high ground."

"Thanks. See ya later!"

Once again I wondered if cats communicate through some form of mental telepathy as they sit, facing each other, for considerable time. Perhaps they try to reach our cluttered minds, only to give up in frustration and resort to body movements, tail positions, and familiar cat sounds.

I reached the edge of the gully and sat down next to Trooper, whose attention was fixed on the culvert. Inside the pipe's entrance crouched two black cats, staring back at us.

I sighed with relief. The cats were the same ones that had disappeared from the feeding area, a mile away.

The pipe where they had apparently been resting for two days was large enough for an average man, walking upright, to pass through with little problem. The purpose of the pipe was to funnel rain water under the road, protecting the asphalt above from flood damage. Although the Vegas Valley area receives only two to four inches of rain a year, when the rain does come, it can be very heavy, rolling across the desert floor and into gullies such as the one bordering our property. The water then moves rapidly through the gullies, then overflowing its banks. But we'd had no recent rain and the sand along the bottom of the pipe was dry.

I stroked Trooper's back. He seemed very tense, but purred anyway. No doubt he was curious about the black cats' intentions. *Where did they come from? Why are they here? Are they after my food?* All the usual questions that must run through the mind of a cat.

Of course, he had no fear of the visitors, being three times their size.

"Oh my goodness!" Chi exclaimed as she reached my side. "I can't believe it. This is a true miracle!"

"Really is," I added, sharing in her happiness.

"I'm so relieved. How did they find us?"

"I think they knew where we lived from the beginning," I answered. "They knew the direction from the sound of the car engine. They heard the car stop. It's almost a mile, but flat. Nothing between here and their feeding spot. Even with their short legs it wasn't such a long journey for cats."

"I hope Trooper didn't harm them. Did he?" Her question was followed by the *pop* sound as she opened the can of cat food. She held the can for Trooper to smell. He turned his head away.

"Trooper hasn't bothered them. He's curious. I guess in cat talk he's asking them what they are doing here."

Chi giggled at my explanation.

I began to explain to Trooper that we were going to feed the visitors and I wanted the three of them to be friends.

According to Herman, the cat standoff had begun at dawn, and it showed no signs of stopping on its own; Trooper had no intention of backing away from his guard position and the black cats had no alternative but to continue to wait in the entrance of the pipe.

I decided to take action and placed the opened can in front of us.

"Come on, girls! This is for you."

Nothing moved.

"OK, Chiaki. You too, Trooper. Let's go to the house."

We began to walk away, and to my surprise, Trooper followed. The standoff had ended.

Moments after we moved, the black cats, who probably had not eaten for two days or even longer, scampered out of the gully and took turns at the can of food.

I slowed my pace and glanced over my shoulder. The two cats were following. Chi and I continued onto the front porch and sat on the top step. Trooper was coming to join us, but in traditional Trooper fashion, was going at his own pace and was in no hurry. He paused now and then to sniff at a leaf or some little thing that attracted his attention. I knew his delaying tactic was to keep the cats at a distance, for when he paused, they stopped as well.

They were about fifteen feet away when Trooper decided it was time for an official introduction. He strolled slowly to the cats, who, despite Trooper's size, did not appear intimidated. They briefly touched noses, then he came and sat down beside me. I wasn't sure how to interpret his gesture, but it obviously was not aggressive. Perhaps they could be friends?

I told my cat that we intended to feed the black cats and they would remain outside until we found them a good home. I guess he understood my intentions because I had already fed them. I knew that Trooper would establish rules and restrictions, as all male cats usually do.

I gradually gave up all hope of companionship between the three felines, as Trooper never accepted the girls as friends, only tolerated them. But we also were to learn that my decision to keep the girls for a while was one of the best decisions I ever made. They would soon play an important role in Trooper's life and, in the process, earn our respect.

I felt a sadness for the cats. They elected to leave their feeding area, forced from it by the construction crews, and gambled to seek safety with us. We were their only hope for survival. They had no way of knowing if we would accept them or turn them out. They had obviously been treated cruelly by the people before. They gave up hope that those evil people would ever return, and now placed their lives in our hands. They were lucky. We are an animal-loving home, and perhaps they sensed that.

So we moved ahead with a plan for the pair to live on the property, at least for a while, until we could find them a loving home. This would continue to be a delicate balance. We needed to care for the girls, but not make Trooper jealous in the process. We gave them both praise and attention, but not when Trooper was near. He always needed to know he remained "top cat; number one!"

Chi suggested I not use the expression "number one" as it might imply that there was a number two or three. She recommended I use "only one" instead. So to make my wife happy I said to Trooper, "You're the only one!" I believe he simply enjoyed any attention and never appeared concerned for his position.

With Trooper's careful inspection, we placed bowls in the shade along the north edge of the driveway, about thirty feet from the front porch—one for water, another for wet food, and a third filled with dry food.

Herman constructed a "cat house" large enough for a big dog, in which we folded an old blanket for the cats' comfort. The house was placed in the shade, a few feet from the food bowls. In all the months the pair lived with us I never noticed them sleeping inside their house, but they did make good use of its slanted roof, which was about four feet above the ground. From that position they safely watched our activity while resting.

Trooper permitted the mother and baby to roam about the property at night, and even let them enter our office through his cat door. They especially appreciated this generosity on those rare nights when it rained. In the morning, before we humans arrived at work, Trooper evicted them and they retreated to shelter in a corner of our front porch.

In order to make them feel even more welcome, we officially gave the pair names: the Persian-looking cat was Mama and the shorthaired one, Baby (I don't think they were actually related).

They came close to us almost every day, but we could not touch them. Any attempt resulted in them backing away. I wasn't surprised by this behavior, considering they must have been traumatized by their previous experiences.

As the two explored the property, I noticed they seemed fascinated with the area to the east, the patch that was cluttered with old farm equipment. Perhaps they felt comfortable in that area, for it was seldom explored by Trooper, or so I had believed.

On hot days Trooper permitted the two to rest under the roof of our portico and on the front porch, and paid no attention to them once they fell asleep.

During those lazy summer days, the sounds of earth-moving equipment leveling the desert a mile to the north reminded us that all evidence of the old golf course was disappearing. Soon the noise of hammers and electric saws announced the construction of new homes.

During those first few days after the pair arrived, the construction noise intensified and my wife expressed concern for the animals left behind. I did my best to convince her that the jackrabbit cleared out before the first bulldozer moved dirt, and the fox family quickly followed.

"The fox is smart," I assured her. "They've gone to a safer place."

"Where?" she pushed.

"Deep in the desert, south of here. There is plenty of open desert to the south where they can hunt."

And that was how, on the fourth day after we adopted the two, a very unusual event occurred which set my wife's mind at ease.

It started with me observing the cats as they followed Trooper about the property on his daily routine inspection. They maintained a distance between themselves and the big cat, and when he stopped, they stopped. When he investigated a tree or bush they waited for him to move on, and then they copied the inspection.

Some who observed this activity would conclude that Trooper requested their company, but knowing my friend, I doubt he did. He was simply demonstrating his system of inspection and the black cats followed, of course, curious and wanting to learn just what Trooper had planned next

Early evening the same day brought an exciting surprise. We finished dinner and decided to stay home to watch the sun sink behind the Spring Mountain's dark silhouette on the western horizon.

Teri closed the office and called on the two-way radio to tell me there were letters on my desk needing my signature. A minute later, Herman radioed that he was conducting his final check of the property.

We opened the front doors and stood, whispering how peaceful our world was at the moment. The distant call of quail scampering to their nest broke the silence. Then the sound faded away.

I was about to turn off my radio and place it in its charger when Herman's voice came through once again.

"Mr. Johnson! Dogs in yard, playing with Trooper!"

Chi and I glanced at each other, our faces reflecting the same question. What dogs? No dogs had visited our ranch before. Then I felt a chill. Could they be coyotes!

I spoke into the radio.

"Herman! Did you say playing? Not fighting?"

"Playing!" came the fast reply. "Chasing each other. Dogs much smaller than Trooper."

"Where?"

"Front yard, near the road."

We could not see ourselves what Herman was reporting because the trees in the front yard blocked our view. We left the porch and started down the driveway towards the road. I heard no growling or cat screams that would indicate a fight was under way. We joined Herman.

"There!" he yelled, pointing to our visitors.

Sitting next to each other, with Trooper standing nearby, were two alert-looking small animals with long, bushy tails. Herman's report was mistaken. The two little animals were not dogs.

Chi tried to control her excitement.

"The foxes!" she shouted enthusiastically. "Both are here!"

Trooper rushed towards me, paused, and then returned to join his new friends. They reacted by running in separate circles, confusing the cat who jerked first left, then right. The larger fox charged at Trooper and rolled over about a foot from the cat. Next, the smaller fox did the same.

This game of attack, chase, fall, and run continued for several minutes as we humans stood, unable to speak. The animals were behaving as if they had been longtime friends and I wondered if Trooper had met them before. It seemed possible, considering their apparent camaraderie.

This confirmed what I had read in the local newspaper. People often report seeing pets playing with a kit fox in their yard. Nevertheless, it was an odd example. Playful creatures who should be enemies in the wild, playing together in domesticity. My wife's eyes flooded with tears of joy.

"How did they find us?" she managed to ask. "First the black cats came and now the fox!"

"I'm sure it was no problem for the fox. They have been hunting the area north of us. I think they knew where we lived, and maybe were concerned about Trooper guarding the property."

"Should I get them some food?" she asked.

"Maybe not. They are just passing by. Let's see what they do next."

It was a comical sight, Trooper, so much larger than the foxes, twisting and turning in circles, creating a moment's blur of dark colored fur.

The larger fox broke from the game, and with his tail pointing parallel to the ground, trotted towards me. He paused a few feet away, his long nose twitching. Then he turned to face the other fox and gave a sharp *yap*.

"Maybe he came to say goodbye," Chi giggled.

"Yeah. Maybe."

Trooper, appearing a little out of breath, came to my side and we watched as the foxes dashed across the road. They paused at the desert's edge, looked back at us, and then trotted into the brush, heading southwest. We walked to the edge of the road and caught a last glimpse of them, bounding over sagebrush.

Then, as it often does in the desert, darkness came quickly.

"They know where to go, to find a new home?" Chi asked.

"Oh, the fox knows," I assured her. "In less than an hour they'll be hunting deep in the desert. It's good. They'll be away from people and all that construction."

"I feel much better now," she said, taking my arm.

"Me too. Come on, cat! Let's go to the house and find you something good to eat."

I was wrapped in a wonderful feeling of contentment as we entered the house. I knew I had been so fortunate to have shared time, even a small part of my life, with wild creatures.

In my office the next morning, I removed a stick from a drawer, the twig the fox presented me not so long ago. I placed it on the desk in front of me and my thoughts tumbled. I had learned one thing from our wildlife encounter. Sometimes we believe we know so much about a friend, but discover we understand so little. When we think we know, we have only unlocked a new mystery.

The foxes were gone, safe somewhere in the desert, and I was happy. But we never saw a fox in our part of the Las Vegas Valley again.

CHAPTER 13

Vanished!

"I believe cats to be spirits come to earth."

Jules Verne

SOME SAY THAT CATS ARE traditionally loners, always spurning the companionship of other felines. In the wild this is generally true, except when cats are playing together as youngsters, or mating as adults. Their territorial instincts are necessary in the wilderness as food supplies are so limited.

Like their wild counterparts, domestic cats are also territorial (and possessive) by nature, but often seek other cats and bond as friends. There are some, of course, who choose to be loners.

We must have found the black cats shortly after they had been abandoned—they could not have survived on their own for long. Surely they were emotionally damaged, but not "wild." But now, they were strangers in a strange place and would not trust humans again for a long time.

Our ranch, with its variety of trees and bushes, provided a safe environment for the pair. They had each other, plenty of food, and some freedom to wander about the property. Trooper enlarged their travel area a little more each week, but Herman's guest house, the office roof, and our home remained off limits for our newest guests.

I spoke to the cats each morning as I walked to the office, and they responded by moving closer to me, only to back away if Trooper appeared on the scene.

One morning in late summer, I didn't see Trooper as I made my way to the office.

"Where's Trooper?" I asked Teri.

"On the roof," Herman responded.

"How does he get up there?"

"He climbs the big pine tree at the east end of the building and jumps onto the roof."

"Oh," I said as I walked back outside.

I stood in the driveway, shielding my eyes from the morning sun with my hand.

It was already hot, and the temperature would reach 110 degrees by 3:00 p.m., as it had the previous day.

"Hi, Trooper! What are you doing up there?"

The cat leaned over the low wall, which ran the entire length of the flat roof. He gave one of his playful gestures by jerking his head to his shoulder, then looked back at me as if to say, "Come on up."

He hopped upon the wall and walked along it until he came to a thick tree branch that hung over the roof. There he leaped out of sight, but had given me a confirmation as to how he reached that vantage point.

"He'll come down when it gets hot," Herman said as he joined me. "Maybe he thinks you'll climb the tree?"

I laughed. "He knows I'm a bad climber. I'm sure he likes it up there. Cats love high places, especially that guy. From there he must have a wonderful view of all our property."

I returned to the office and was interrupted, again, by Herman, who announced, "Trooper down now. He saw something interesting."

"Really. What?"

"Don't know. He ran fast towards the southeast corner of the yard."

"Spotted a rabbit, I bet," Teri chimed in.

Chi and I went to our gift shop that evening, returning a little after midnight. The black cats were waiting for us near the front porch. We gave them some fresh food and water and retired. It had been a busy day, and I was exhausted.

The next morning as I awoke, I realized that Trooper did not come to bed during the night. But had I slept so soundly I simply did not feel his presence? In the kitchen I discovered his food had not been touched. I assumed he found something interesting during the night and would return for food later in the day.

"Trooper come out here this morning?" I inquired as I entered the office.

No one responded.

By the end of the day he still had not returned for food. Chi and I discussed the events around the last time he disappeared.

The next day yielded no Trooper. I decided that if he did not return on the third day I would take some steps to find him. Thus, on that day I organized my first "search party." The team consisted of Herman, Teri, two of her friends, and myself. We gathered shortly before noon and tested the two-way radios.

The black cats approached our group and sat down, staring at us.

"They sure are curious," Teri noted.

"Yeah," I answered, "and this is kind of odd. They never came close to strangers before."

"Maybe they want to join us," Teri said, "or . . . maybe they know something."

"I doubt it. They are simple cats."

My plan was to first search the southern boundary of the property. This would include the gully where small trees and tangled vines presented a great place for a cat to play or hide.

As I entered the gully I thought of an old saying, something my grandmother once told me: If a cat doesn't want to be found, you'll not find him. The gully, several feet deep in some places, with sloping side walls, had bottom soil that felt dry and soft beneath our feet. We found no sign of Trooper, no fur left on underbrush, no footprints . . . nothing.

Someone mentioned rattlesnakes. Could the cat have become a victim of a snake bite? I tried to force that thought from my mind. There are two venomous snakes on our ranch. The most feared in the Las Vegas Valley is the Mojave green rattlesnake, so named for the reptile's medium-green body with diamond-shaped markings on its back. It is small, and its bite, with dispensing fangs delivering venom, can be deadly to animals the size of a coyote (or bobcat), though less than one percent of humans die after being bitten.

The other rattlesnake feared in our valley is the sidewinder, named for its side-winding locomotion. It can reach a length of thirty inches, but its venom is almost as lethal as that of the Mojave green. One of the characteristics of the sidewinder, which makes it especially dangerous, is the ability to bury itself in loose sand, dust, or gravel and hide, waiting patiently for its next victim.

I didn't know if Trooper had encountered a rattlesnake before; I had to assume with all his exploring that he had. At least, to that day, he had never been bitten. I worried that due to the well-known curiosity of my cat, he might be attracted to and investigate the buzzing sound of the snake's rattle. Would instinct keep him out of danger when the snake lunged to strike? The snake's strike is fast, but the cat may be faster.

And then I remembered the time, several years before, when I scolded Trooper for stalking the great snake killer, the funny-acting bird known as the road runner. The cat, fascinated by the long-legged bird's movements, had indicated a desire to catch it. But with the ability to reach running speeds of over twenty-five miles per hour, the bird neatly outdistanced the cat, and when Trooper did close in, it lowered its feathered crest and flew a short distance. The road runner, with its long tail, has a clownish gait on the ground, and often, after his brief flight, tumbles when landing like a clumsy acrobat. Then it springs to its feet and, with a shake of feathers, runs again. It appears, as it spends so much time on the ground and flies so seldom, to forget how to land gracefully. It was no wonder that the cat found this bird interesting, but quickly learned that it could only be caught by doing what he did best, waiting and attacking from ambush. This I discouraged, and I never found evidence that he had killed a road runner.

The road runner is found throughout the Southwest, Northern Mexico, and on our ranch. Although the road runner is only twenty-four inches long, it is feared by rattlesnakes, which it hunts on a regular basis. The bird eats scorpions, mice, lizards, and spiders, but snakes are a favorite meal.

Using its wings like a matador's cape, the bird torments the rattlesnake while judging its striking ability. The runner, three times faster than the attacking snake, leaps and snatches it in his long bill. Then the bird slams the snake upon a rock or hard ground several times, killing it.

Though popular as a snake killer, he is perhaps best known as the cartoon character who consistently outruns his animated nemesis, Wile E. Coyote, in Looney Tunes.

That night we gathered again, this time to manufacture posters, which were to be attached to telephone poles, fence posts, and trees in our area, with special attention to cross streets where vehicles either slowed or came to a complete stop.

The poster read:

LOST

Large brown cat with short tail
BIG CASH REWARD
Name – Trooper
No questions asked.

Our phone number appeared at the end.

The black kitties greeted me once again as I walked to the office the next morning. They circled around me several times, apparently enjoying new freedom without Trooper.

Teri informed me that thirty posters were already up, and some had been placed on mailboxes along our road for almost a mile. She placed an ad in the *Las Vegas Review-Journal* lost and found section of the classifieds, but I held little hope that it would yield any good news.

We sent a copy of the ad by fax to Doctor Marg and every veterinarian hospital within a four-mile radius of our home. Our thinking was that someone might find the cat and take him to a nearby clinic. And, of course, we also contacted the private animal shelters, as well as one run by the county.

Another day, and then another, passed. On the sixth day since Trooper went missing, using ideas from my time in the Army, I organized our helpers into squads and assigned them to sections I had marked on a geological map. The desert south of the gully was the next to be searched. After lunch we planned to comb the rough land to the west beyond the road in front of our property. I knew Trooper often used the culvert pipe to cross under the road to that area.

While my volunteers were searching there, I walked down the road to visit Jim Butler. The old man, using his golf cart, traveled about the neighborhood, spending time with friends, sharing information and local gossip.

On the way to Jim's, I encountered the rural mail carrier and waved for him to stop his white jeep. He already knew about our cash reward offered for the cat and assured me he would stay alert for him.

I was relieved to see the golf cart sitting in Jim's driveway.

"I know your cat is missing," he said. "Got your ad in my mailbox."

"Have you heard anything from your friends down the road that might be helpful?"

"Nope," came the fast reply, his stern face reflecting no emotion. "Seems like everyone knows about your cat. No one seen him recently. I told you that wild animals like your cat often return to the wilderness . . . going back to where they came from. You can't blame them. It's in their blood to be wild. Maybe that's what your friend has done. All your love and attention can't stop the urge. Be happy for him; you gave him the freedom and he had to take it! But . . ." Jim paused. "I think he'll come back, maybe just to visit. You are part of each other."

"Yes," I replied, quite disturbed by his answer and attitude.

"You got to accept the fact that he may leave again. You understand?"

My mind struggled to forget his comments. I could not think of Trooper simply leaving me. We had slept together, had eaten together, had played together. I wanted to believe we were the same, that we had bonded like brothers. I didn't think the cat even knew he was once wild. Had my feelings all been much too human? I had to be realistic, force myself to agree: wild was in his blood.

"Coyotes are my biggest concern," I managed to say in an effort to hide my true feelings.

"Those damn predators!" Jim exclaimed. "You know, about a week ago, my friend Roger, he lives a mile south of here, he was driving home one night. His headlights caught four coyotes in the middle of the road. They had surrounded a cat. It weren't yours, a much smaller, regular cat. The coyotes were closing in on that poor cat. Nowhere for him to run. Couldn't break out of the circle. Roger stopped and got out of the car, cursing the fact that he left his gun at home. He yelled at the coyotes. They paid no attention. So he picked up a few big rocks from the side of the road and began throwing at them coyotes. Hit one in the head. They all ran off into the darkness."

"And the cat?"

"Oh," Jim laughed, "you know cats. He was a lucky one, he was. When the attack broke off, the cat bounded over a wall and escaped. I'm telling you, we'll get those predators someday. If they come in this yard they are gonna get shot!"

I thanked Jim and started for home, my thoughts floating to something Doctor Marg once said. "He'll find his way home if he's physically capable." This vibrated in my mind, and I convinced myself once more: Trooper did not run away to the wild. He was not a victim of a coyote attack or a snake bite. He had to be trapped somewhere, but where?

At home the black cats circled around me again, making it difficult to avoid tripping over them.

Herman was waiting at the office door. He reported that the morning search found no signs of Trooper.

"Let's try the desert to the north, all the way to the construction site. I'll take an ad or two to the workers. Maybe they have seen him."

I left the search teams and drove to the construction area. To my surprise, the workers I spoke with were sympathetic, one kindly sharing, "We'll watch for him, pal. No one likes losing a pet."

On the morning of the seventh day without Trooper, a team of a dozen people were waiting at my office. They said they all had met Trooper before while visiting us, had pets of their own, and wanted to help.

I thanked all of them for donating their time, and was very moved emotionally by their concern. I promised a quick lunch and cold drinks for everyone. I suggested we discontinue the search by 1:00 p.m. as the heat would make extended exercise very danger-ous. Weathermen predicted 115 degrees by midafternoon.

I divided the group into squads once more and issued two-way radios and bottled water. I wanted to search the gully and areas in all directions for at least two hundred yards. We must discontinue the search by 1 or 2 p.m.

Someone inquired into searching our neighbor's yard to the east, but both Teri and Herman thought that that would be a waste of time. They had never seen Trooper enter the area, so it was un-likely that he'd be there now. Vines, high grass, and thorny sage, tangled with old tractors, made it almost impossible for one to enter the yard from our property. *Maybe impossible for a person, but what about a cat*, I questioned. They doubted that also.

I joined the team on the way to search the gully. My thoughts were on the last time Trooper vanished. That duration was only three days. Now we were at one week. If he was trapped somewhere he could not survive much longer without food and water.

Suddenly the black baby cat darted between my legs, then ran in front of me and sat down.

"What's wrong with you girls?" I snapped at the cats. "You've been acting crazy lately!"

She turned and shot a glance at me over her shoulder. Mama cat joined her, stared at me several seconds, and then the two began to walk towards the southeast corner of the property. They stopped again and waited.

A strange feeling crawled through me. Something told me— only a quick thought, but a strong one—they were speaking to me. I heard nothing. But I felt a chill, then warm all over.

Silly, I thought. Of course I felt warm. It was a hot day, a very hot day.

The girls continued on to the gully. There they paused and came next to me. For the first time they let me reach out and stroke their soft black fur. It was warm from the sun.

"What is it, girls?" I asked. Again, only silence.

They left me there on the edge of our property wondering just what they were trying to tell me. Did they really know something important, or were they only funny cats seeking attention?

CHAPTER 14

Rescue!

"I wish I could write as mysterious as a cat."

Edgar Allen Poe

WHERE WAS MY CAT? WE entered the seventh day of his disappearance and still had seen neither head nor tail of him, and had no leads, either. My wife sympathized with my frustration and sadness, suggesting I should give up hope, accept the fact that he was gone, and accept that we might never know what happened to him. But I wasn't going to give up with my faith and hope that I would find Trooper alive. I refused to surrender my belief that he was still alive, somewhere.

I sat in my office the morning of Trooper's eighth day away from home, my feet propped up on the desk, contemplating my next effort towards finding my cat. Concentration was difficult. My thoughts had become saturated with memories of Trooper. I know that this often happens when one loses something or someone dear. Memories become part of the healing process.

Two weeks before he went missing, I recalled an incident that, although forgettable at the time, seemed important now. Trooper was sleeping, as he so often did, on my desk across from me. He suddenly became alert, with eyes wide and ears pointing towards the closed door. He sat up, his short tail twitching.

I heard no sound, yet the cat knew something was on the other side of that door. He leaped silently to the floor, walked towards the door, and then paused.

I opened the door. The mama cat sat on the opposite side of the driveway, about fifty feet away. The two cats stared at each other for three minutes, neither making a sound nor moving a muscle.

How did my sleeping Trooper know that the black cat waited outside?

"Do you want to try another search, Dad?" Teri's question abruptly snapped me out of my daydream.

"What?" I replied.

"Are you giving up?"

"Not completely," I said, "but I can't think of a place we haven't checked. Can you, Herman?"

The old German stroked his pointed chin, which often remained rigid when he spoke.

"We have looked everywhere," he responded. "Twice in some places."

"Another search of the desert really won't accomplish anything." I said. "I'm running out of ideas. No response from our posters, no phone calls."

"So, what's next? What can we do to help?" asked Teri.

"Nothing right now," I replied resignedly. "Go on with your work. I'm taking a walk. Got to think. I'll take my radio so call me if something interesting comes in."

I knew, from my years of exploring our desert, that it is impossible to cover an area completely. From above, the desert floor appears flat, void of any obstructions. Of course, it is not flat. At ground level one discovers the terrain to be rolling with small hills, the earth buckled by millions of years of erosion and movement.

Dry washes or dry creek beds, gullies and ravines, often hidden by sage, creosote bushes, and desert willow trees crisscross the land. Cacti of all sorts add to the difficulty and danger of traversing those rugged areas.

We could not cover its entirety in just two searches or even in two hundred.

As I walked a few paces from the office, I stumbled over the baby cat, who rushed between my legs out of a hiding place. I regained my pace only to feel her brush against my leg while crying frantically with meows. At first I thought I might have injured her when I tripped, but that was not her problem.

She dashed in front of me, then returned, crying loudly, and repeated the odd behavior as I walked on at a steady pace. Finally I realized she was trying to lead me into the side yard. When I followed, her crying instantly diminished.

Did she really have something to show me, or as I previously thought, was this was only a simple cat, seeking attention?

"Didn't we make this trip before?" I said to the cat, exasperated. "The last time you left me sitting in the yard, if you recall!"

But this time, she led me farther across the yard in the direction of the gully. At the corner of the property we encountered Mama cat. At this point, I was convinced that the two had something that they considered important to share with me. But would it be important to me, or did they simply want to play? I decided to go along with them just in case they really had something to show me.

They both began to meow as they continued on into the gully. We traveled east several yards. The cats were silent now, apparently convinced they had my attention.

I followed slowly until we reached the edge of my neighbor's property. There, Baby turned to the left and started into that yard in a northern direction, entering a small tunnel in the brush, probably created by rabbits. Mama fell behind, sat down, and watched as I fought my way through vines and tall sage, attempting to keep track of her baby.

I felt the sting as thorns cut my jeans and ripped my thin cotton shirt, but I moved on, trying to keep up with the cat. She paused occasionally to look back, as if to check on my progress.

I lost her for a few moments. *Which way did she go? Did she turn or continue straight? How stupid*, I thought. I had no idea why I should be following a cat, an animal I barely knew, into that jungle.

I considered turning back and letting the cats play together as they desired. But then, suddenly, I broke free of the tangled mess and found myself standing at the edge of a clearing, which was invisible from the direction we came. The cat was waiting for me a few feet away.

"OK," I said, "now what?"

She looked at me, gave a pleasant-sounding meow, and moved past, entering the brush directly behind me. Apparently we had reached our destination. *What was so important about this spot? Why did she need to share it with me?* So there I stood, feeling foolish to have followed a cat to nowhere interesting.

My eyes searched the clearing in hopes of spotting something that I had missed. The area had freshly cut grass in contrast to the jungle-like terrain we crossed. That flat land continued some sixty or seventy feet to my neighbor's old barn, against which leaned a variety of rusting plow blades. I sighed, took in a deep breath, and started to reenter the brush and fight my way through it. I simply wanted to return home.

Then I heard something. Something that sounded like an animal crying. More specifically, an animal I knew well crying.

"Trooper!" I shouted, desperately grasping at the hope that he was nearby.

And then a louder cry! Not the strong scream I often heard from my cat, but a weak facsimile.

How stupid I had been. The black cat knew Trooper was in this area. They attempted to show me days before, but I didn't trust them. I thought they were simply little animals trying to seek attention.

"Trooper! Where are you?"

I was frantic. My heart pounded as I rushed to the barn. I reached the door. A large padlock secured it. I moved to the north end of the building, not knowing what I expected to find. I had to locate another entrance!

I heard the cry again, this time much stronger.

"Trooper! Where . . ."

My shout was interrupted by a yowling sound coming from above. I looked up. There, almost ten feet above my head, I saw his face, pressed against a jagged hole in the boards. Apparently he had managed to enlarge an opening by scratching at the thick oak wood until he could force his face through. It was still much too small for his head.

My first thought was, *How do I get him out of the barn?* And then, *how did he get inside a locked barn in the first place?*

"Hold on Trooper! I'll get help."

I rushed back to the door and pulled on the padlock. The lock and the thick metal guard on the wood around it were both strong. I needed a heavy hammer and chisel or crowbar to break it open.

But I had no right to destroy someone's property, even if it was to save my friend. If I was caught, regardless of my intention, I could be arrested.

I started to press the radio button and call Herman for help. He had the necessary tools to break into the place and the knowledge to do it easily. Then a better idea hit me. Maybe the owner was home or someone there knew the location of the key. If not, then breaking in would be the necessary resort.

I spoke to Trooper with a shaky voice, assuring him I would return, and then ran to the front of the house. An elderly lady answered the doorbell. I frantically introduced myself and explained, "My cat is trapped in your barn! He's been in there for a week with no food or water! Do you have a key?"

"Oh, yes!" she exclaimed. "My husband always keeps that door locked. How did your cat get in there?"

"I have no idea!"

"He keeps it locked because he's afraid vandals will get in and destroy the place."

"Yes, I understand. Do you have a key? I can get my cat . . ."

She finally recognized my desperation.

"Yes, yes. He keeps it on a nail in the kitchen wall."

She returned faster than I expected, and we walked together to the barn.

Along the way she said, "I just remembered. My husband was out here doing something about a week ago. At dinner, that night, he said he thought he may have forgotten to close and lock that door. He came out here in the dark to lock the place up. Been open all day, he said."

I remembered Herman reporting more than a week ago that Trooper came down from the office roof and rushed to the southeast corner of our property. Nothing unusual about that, but from his position, high up on the roof, he might have seen the open door on the barn, a door that was always closed before then. Without a doubt, this would have been a great temptation for the cat. A closed door tends to bother cats, and if open, the inside demands inspection. Or he could have simply discovered the opening while exploring that mysterious yard. Either way, he went inside the barn and the husband returned and locked the door, not realizing he had trapped a visitor inside.

The key worked! The lock sprang and I had the door completely open.

The barn had no windows, or if it did, they were boarded up, preventing light from entering. The only light came as a glow above a wide shelf, a hole the cat had clawed in the thick boards.

Suddenly, I heard a sound, like something falling. A metallic sound, perhaps a can of some sort. And then the sound of wood rubbing against wood.

"Trooper!" I managed to shout but in a very subdued voice. "I'm here, Troop. Where are you?"

I was answered with silence.

My eyes strained, but could not focus in on anything. My throat was dry and my legs felt like they were paralyzed, unable to move in any direction. I tried to lean forward and reach into that black room, but what for? What did I expect to grasp when I could see nothing?

Suddenly, from somewhere in the darkness, Trooper leaped onto my chest. The impact caught me by surprise and knocked me backward. My arms quickly wrapped around him and my eyes flooded. He was purring loudly.

"My, he's a big kitty!" the lady remarked as I handed her the key.

"Thank you," I managed to say. Nothing more was needed. My face said it all.

"Let's go home, Troop!"

He began to squirm and jumped from my arms. I tried to follow as we rushed through the hellish underbrush. I managed to keep up with him, ignoring the thorns cutting through my shirt, until we reached the gully. At our backyard he broke into a full run in the direction of the house. I didn't try to race with him. That was impossible.

In the excitement I had forgotten the radio. I removed it from my belt, pushed the button, and shouted:

"I found Trooper! He's OK! We're running to the house now."

Teri was the first to reply, "Thank God! I'll see you guys at the house."

The black cats were lying in the shade next to the back porch as Trooper darted through his cat door and into the kitchen.

I paused as I reached the steps and looked at the girls.

"Thank you," I said. "I'll tell Trooper . . . I'll tell everyone you girls saved him."

Chi stood next to Trooper as he lapped up water from his bowl.

"I heard your radio call," she said, while dabbing at tears with a paper towel. "I can't believe he's still alive."

Teri joined us, shaking her head in disbelief.

"The black cats showed me where you were, Trooper," I said to the unresponsive cat.

He turned and looked up at me as if to ask, "What took you so long?" Then he walked towards the bedroom.

"He didn't eat," Chi noted.

"I guess he knows what he needs. He's stressed out. We all are. I'm sure he'll eat later. We'll let him rest and take him to visit Doctor Marg in the morning, when he is more relaxed."

I went to the bedroom and climbed on top of the blanket to be next to my cat. He pushed his head under my arm and began to purr. We both fell into a contented sleep.

That evening he enjoyed a full can of wet food, a little of his dry food, and washed it all down with a quantity of water. He journeyed outside briefly, but returned in an hour to nap on a living room chair.

The next morning, we managed to get him into his travel crate with surprisingly little pushback, although he did grumble on the way to the animal hospital.

"What has this fellow been up to this time?" Doctor Marg greeted us with a smile as she picked up the cat and placed him on the exam table. She then began to massage his body.

Trooper remained peaceful. He loved Doctor Marg, although he hated the trip required to visit her.

I related the details of his disappearance and rescue as she checked his heart with a stethoscope. Then she turned her attention to Trooper's thick file.

"He's ten years old!" she announced, as if a little surprised. "You're a senior citizen cat."

"The years have gone by in a flash," I added.

"Trooper, you gave up another life," she said. "You must have six remaining . . . or is it five? I can't remember."

"I lost count," I confessed, with a slight laugh.

"Based on your story, I think the black cats, as you call them, must have known where he was trapped. Undoubtedly they heard his cries from the beginning. Cats have such a strong sense of hearing. You and your friends simply couldn't hear him at a distance, added to the fact that he called from inside a building with thick walls. I'll do my best to find a home for those cats."

"They deserve a good home," I concurred.

"I know you and your cat have both been under a lot of stress," she said, "but I don't think there is anything physically wrong with him. Maybe lost a pound or a little more. That would be like you losing ten pounds. So give him his usual food and he'll gain it all back at his own pace. Wild cats often go a long time without food or water, especially those in the desert. Of course, your boy has been a little spoiled, to say the least. But his genes pulled him through this time."

I thanked her and with Trooper back in his crate was ready to pay the bill at the front desk. I paused as the doctor spoke again.

"You know, Mr. Johnson, I considered retiring this year. I have a potential buyer for the business. But customers like you two help keep my work interesting."

"And rewarding," I jokingly injected

She smiled and replied, "Of course. Very rewarding. Take care of your friend. You have done a wonderful job so far."

I told her how much I would appreciate her finding the black cats a home. I knew they would never be comfortable as outside cats. But I had one stipulation: the two must remain together.

I have no way of knowing if Trooper thanked the black cats for leading me to him that day, or if he understood anything about the events up to the moment of rescue. Do animals thank one another or reward with special favors as we humans often do?

I can, however, relate unusual events that occurred that winter, a few months after the rescue.

December is always a cold month in the Mojave Desert, and that year the plunging temperatures broke records. At night it usually fell to the low forties, but it hit eighteen degrees and high winds brought dangerous chill factors. The bitter cold lasted less than two weeks, but the thermometer hung at the freezing mark much longer.

During those cold nights Trooper did little roaming outside, electing instead to curl up in front of the wood-burning fireplace or on the blankets of my bed.

We worried about the black cats outside and added an extra fluffy blanket to their cardboard box, which we placed in the corner of the front porch, out of the wind. But this provided little protection from the freezing temperatures.

On the second cold night, around 9 p.m., I heard a series of meows in the front of the house. Since Trooper doesn't meow, I knew the sound was obviously coming from another cat. I left my bed and walked to the living room to investigate. No cats there.

I turned and looked into the dining room. Trooper sat, facing one of the chairs. There, appearing both comfortable and warm on the chair's soft cushion, was Mama. Baby rested in the chair next to her. They both stared at me, perhaps worried I might force them to go outside.

So Trooper had moved jealousy and territorial concerns aside and eliminated our worry for the cats' safety. He had led the pair inside, and to our surprise, allowed them to remain there all night.

When the sun warmed the morning air, the two returned to their outside world. But the sleeping arrangement continued until winter yielded to a balmy spring.

I complimented the cat for his compassion and have always wondered, *were those warm, inside nights his way of rewarding them?*

CHAPTER 15

The Night Visitor

"Everything in kitty's world belongs to kitty."

Old English Proverb

THE SALESMAN SAT WITH A rigid, military-like bearing in the chair opposite my desk, waiting for me to make a decision on how many monogrammed polo shirts to purchase for our gift shop.

We exchanged polite conversation on other subjects from time to time as we had in previous business meetings, but I always had to pay close attention to understand, as his words were heavy with a Chinese accent. His merchandise was, however, of good quality and priced competitively. I only needed to make a decision on the exact quantity to buy.

While we discussed delivery time we were interrupted by a horn blowing in the driveway. He responded to the puzzled look on my face.

"Mother, father wait in car. They from China. Visit me in LA."

"Oh," I responded. "Why don't we invite them in? They could join us for something to drink; a soda perhaps. I didn't know you had anyone with you."

"They don't speak English," the salesman said, "only Chinese."

"That's OK," I replied, "maybe they will be more comfortable . . ."

The horn sounded again, a longer blast this time. Then the salesman's cell phone rang. A brief conversation followed in Chinese. A strange look dominated his face as he closed the phone and stared at me, eyes wide.

"Father say . . . large wild animal trying to get in car!" he said, with a slight element of doubt in his voice.

We rushed out the office door. There in the driveway was a blue compact car. Trooper sat on the hood, his face only inches from the windshield. He had one of his large fuzzy paws pressed against the glass.

"That's my pet cat. He won't hurt them," I assured him, "he's only curious."

The salesman approached the side window and shouted words of comfort to his parents through the glass. The elderly couple did not appear convinced.

"Here," I said, "come over here next to me and touch the cat. His name is Trooper. Maybe your parents will understand that the cat is harmless."

He came to my side and reluctantly stroked Trooper's back. Then he returned to the side window and spoke to his father again. The old man answered, and nodded his head with a slight smile.

"Father say, 'thank you very much', but . . . they will wait in car. Been in USA three days. Never seen cat that big. Me also."

"Trooper is a funny cat," I said as we returned to the office. "He is possessive. He believes everything on this property, including cars, belongs to him. He investigates all visitors."

Our business meeting ended in a friendly manner.

Trooper's possessiveness was never-ending. Non-living things, such as automobiles, concerned him less than living creatures, especially humans who entered his territory. Though often shy, his curiosity was nevertheless apparent. Protecting his world remained his responsibility, a serious assignment assumed, actually, by all cats.

Felines often sleep sixteen to eighteen hours a day and must rely on their keen senses to perform their duties. Beyond the usual sight, smell, and hearing, the cat has yet another sense he can depend upon. That intangible is the natural instinct of feeling something, especially danger, is near. This will tell the cat to flee, stand and fight, or hide. If none of those apply, he will investigate. Naturally, the longer a cat has lived "in the wild," or the more time he has spent outside, the keener this instinct.

It was a beautiful, warm night in October. A full moon projected a glow on the desert floor and beams flooded through our windows like mellow floodlights on a stage. We retired early, and in my haste to enjoy a full night's sleep, I made one dangerous mistake: I forgot to activate the alarm system, which was designed to emit a shrill, heart-stopping siren if a door or window opened, or if someone over four feet tall moved about the room. Activating the alarm required the simple task of someone pushing two buttons on a keypad located near the front door. Another keypad was on the wall in our bedroom, but for some unknown reason, I paid no attention to it that night.

So we fell asleep, oblivious to the possible danger my negligence might have caused.

Trooper, free as always to venture out his cat door, was outdoors somewhere, unlocking mysteries in dark shadows. Sometime after midnight he usually came to our bed to sleep at my feet or snuggle under my arm. I awoke each time the twenty-eight-pound cat jumped into bed. My wife always continued to sleep peacefully.

That October night had been an especially restless one for me. I slept lightly and had no purring cat next to me. Perhaps my brain was trying to tell me to get up and turn on the alarm.

Suddenly I awoke to a strange noise. It came from the narrow hall that connects our bedroom and the front of the house. It sounded as if a fat man was having difficulty squeezing between the walls. Then, a series of thumping sounds. I was wide awake and reaching for my .45 automatic in the drawer of the bedside table. I slid back the receiver, loading the first round.

From the dark hall came a loud scream followed by a growl. Trooper! There was no other creature that a scream like that could have come from. But what had caused his alarm?

I glanced at the clock: 2 a.m.

My wife was now awake.

"What is it?" she whispered.

"Don't know. Trooper must have something trapped in the hall."

"Oh," she gasped. "I didn't set the alarm. Did you?"

"No," I confessed, "I forgot."

"Oh, no!"

I grasped her arm. "Get your cell and slide out of bed as quietly as possible. Stay on the floor and keep the bed between you and the doorway! Be ready to call 911."

"Yes," she answered as she rolled from the bed.

I moved towards the open door, pistol in hand. There had been no more noise from the hall for almost two minutes, but then the thumping sound began again.

"I'm going to check it out," I announced in a low voice. "I'm sure it is Trooper . . . at least I think it is, with something."

"Or someone," she added.

That thought gave me a cold chill. With the alarm system deactivated, Trooper could, indeed, have someone against the wall.

"If I shoot or yell, you call 911, and stay on your side of the bed. If anyone comes through that doorway . . . that's not me, you lay flat. Understand!?"

"Yes."

Then another scream in the hall followed by a sound I had never heard before. It was more of a screech than a scream.

My left hand moved along the wall, seeking the light switch. I found it, but hesitated.

The thought that someone might be in the hall with the cat made me pause and take a deep breath. I raised the pistol, pointed it into the darkness, and flipped the switch.

"Oh my gosh!" I exclaimed.

There, blocking the hallway between the cat and me, was a very large bird, its wings extending wall to wall and partially blocking a view of Trooper. But I could see that the cat was crouched in his leap-and-attack position, mouth wide and open, exposing his long teeth in a threatening snarl.

His enemy had a barreled shape, a feathered body, and stood almost two feet tall.

"Wait, Trooper!" I shouted.

The bird turned his head towards me and blinked large yellow eyes. At once I knew he was an owl, a very angry one.

"What is it?" my wife called.

"An owl!"

"What? Did you say owl?"

"I think he's a horned owl—the biggest one I have ever seen."

"How did an owl get in our hall?"

"Don't know," I answered. "Trooper must have caught him and he's bringing him in to show us."

She peeked around the doorway. "My! He's huge!" she announced with excitement.

I pushed her back gently.

"Careful," I warned. "Don't get close—this guy can be dangerous. He has strong, sharp talons. I don't know how the cat got him this far without a fight."

"He is sooo beautiful," was her reply. "How are you going to get him to leave?"

"I've got an idea," I said, placing the pistol on the floor. "He's not going to leave without our encouragement. Get me a thin, lightweight blanket from the closet."

She was at my side in a few moments and handed me the blanket.

"I think the hall light has him blinded. I hope so! But he has great hearing and can detect movement so we've got to act fast."

"OK . . . and do what?"

Trooper began to growl and hiss loudly. He was answered by a high-pitched screech from the owl.

"No! Trooper. Don't attack!" I ordered the cat.

"I'll throw this blanket over the bird," I said. "When I yell, you run to the front, open the double doors, and turn off the porch light. I'll grab the bundle with the owl and get him out the front door. Hopefully, he'll head to the darkness. Ready?"

"Yes."

I tossed the blanket. Quite luckily, it fell atop the owl, covering his body completely. I quickly gathered the blanket around him, taking care not to harm his wings, which he began to retract.

"Run!" I shouted.

The cat turned and darted down the hall, slid across the marble foyer, recovered, and waited at the door for Chi, who followed closely behind him.

Chi opened the double doors and turned off the lights as I scooped up the owl and rushed to the porch. The owl remained still as I carefully uncovered him. Then I stood back a few feet and waited.

My wife, the cat, and I watched as the feathered visitor turned his head for one last look at his captors. His yellow eyes blinked and he faced the darkness of our front yard.

His wings opened, raised, and then lowered, as if being tested. Then they flapped a few times as he lifted from the porch and flew quietly some twenty or thirty feet, parallel to the ground, clearly visible in the moonlight.

At this point, his flight reminded me of scenes of World War II fighter planes leaving an aircraft carrier deck. The bird banked left, then right, then glided gracefully, silently between two pine trees and disappeared into the night.

We stood, as if hypnotized by the flight of the owl, grappling with the thought that this was really happening. Somehow it seemed as if I had dreamed the entire evening's event, especially the beautiful, quiet flight of the owl. For a moment I felt I was flying with him. What a thrill it would be to sail through the night sky so effortlessly. That dream quickly faded, but it had been a wonderful experience with a happy ending.

"He'll sure have a story to tell his family." Chi broke the silence.

"Right! Now we can find out how Trooper caught him and managed to get the bird all the way down the hall with no damage to either one of them."

Trooper stared at me with an inquisitive look and said nothing. But I could feel him asking, "What was it?"

"That was a horned owl—the strongest predator in our sky. How did you catch him?"

The cat looked away and did not answer.

"He flies so quietly, not a sound," Chi said. "Thank you, Trooper, for not killing him."

"Trooper had no intention to kill the bird," I said. "If he had, he would have done so before he brought him in and there would be a big pile of feathers out here somewhere."

"We can investigate after sunrise," Chi said. "Let's get some sleep."

"OK," I agreed. "Come on, Troop. We've had a busy night."

Trooper followed us into the bedroom, pausing only to smell a tiny feather left in the hall by our visitor.

"In a little while, you can show me where you caught the owl," I said to the cat.

Trooper did not respond. He was already asleep under my arm.

I awoke shortly after sunrise, anxious to solve the night's mysteries. I fixed a cup of coffee and strolled to the front door. Trooper was there, stretched out on the red tile. As I neared, he stood, stretched, and shook himself. Dust flew from his fur, revealing he had already rolled in the desert dirt.

It's a surprisingly little known fact that all cats roll in the dirt, if given the opportunity. Rolling seems to come as an impulse, but I learned from an old prospector that wild cats—bobcats and mountain lions—use the dust to reduce the sheen of a glossy coat that reflects sun or moonlight. The reflection could alert an enemy, or warn a prey. But after a few active hours most of the dust is gone from the coat. For some cats, the rolling exercise is nothing more than instinct. With others, especially wild cats, it is both instinct and a planned event executed for a valuable reason. The owl had entered the cat's world. To Trooper, the bird belonged to him. So the "why" he captured the owl was understood. The "how" remained the mystery.

"Come on, Trooper. Let's find out where you caught the owl."

The cat followed me slowly to the walkway that ran next to the east side of our home. He flopped down on the concrete beneath his cat door located directly under a large picture window and rolled a few times.

What was he trying to tell me? *Asleep? Ridiculous!* I laughed. Owls don't take naps on a sidewalk in the middle of the night. There were, however, a few feathers scattered about on the concrete revealing that something had occurred there.

Trooper sat and with an alert expression, stared up at the window. The window had been tinted years ago by the previous owner to reflect the brilliant morning sun rays. From the outside where we were it appeared as a large, dark mirror. At night it simply looked like a big, black hole in the wall.

Suddenly one mystery was solved. A perfect silhouette, a picture print of a large bird with wings outstretched, was there in the dust on the blackened glass.

The owl apparently had flown into the glass, not realizing it was a closed window. A feather was stuck on the glass in the center of the silhouette. And there was the answer: The bird smashed, while in flight, into the glass, knocking himself out and falling to the sidewalk, unconscious. That was how Trooper found him.

Trooper brushed against my leg for attention.

"How did you get the owl through your door?" I asked the cat. "It's only wide enough for you."

Trooper watched me with a blank expression. I reached to touch the entrance of the cat's hole in the wall and he rubbed the side of his head on my hand. "You must have pushed the bird through the hole. There is no other way."

I began to laugh as I visualized the scene, since the bird was almost Trooper's size. While Trooper had plenty of strength, he would have needed all of it to accomplish such a feat, and he still had had to carry or pull the owl down the hall.

"You're lucky he didn't wake up until he did," I teased. "You would have had a battle on your paws!" But the bird did wake en route to our bedroom, and that was when all the noise began. I stooped to scratch the cat between his ears.

"Thank you for sharing your beautiful owl with us," I said.

I don't think Trooper noticed me smiling as I spoke, as he was already strolling towards the edge of his domain. Through it all he pretended the previous night had been nothing more than a routine occurrence. So it is with cats. But of course, my wife and I felt differently.

After that, a month went by. Our neighbor across the road reported that a large owl had been resting in his tree a few nights each week. Apparently Trooper's acquaintance had found a new hunting ground, for he never visited us again.

CHAPTER 16

The Bodyguard

"Some say man is the most dangerous animal on the planet. Obviously those people have never met an angry cat."

Lillian Johnson

I STROLLED SLOWLY FROM OUR little office building to the front porch, breathing in the early morning desert air. It was crisp and clean, and my lungs cherished every breath. A light breeze carried the sweet scent of wild sage, and when I turned to look past the front yard and circular driveway onto the country road, all seemed still.

Often I made that thirty-yard journey wrapped up in daydreams that I quickly forgot. But that morning my breathing was somewhat labored and I was preoccupied with worries that my asthma might give me problems later in the day. I felt confident, however, with a new emergency inhaler given to me by my doctor a few days before.

Trooper was stretched out on the red-tile porch enjoying a nap in the morning sun. His fur absorbed the warm sun rays. His short tail twitched and his big ears moved slightly, acknowledging my presence. He hadn't been asleep, only resting after a long night of patrolling his territory. *How quiet he is*, I thought, *not even snoring*. No one would ever guess that this little animal's scream could make the hair on the back of the neck stand up; no one, that is, except those who have wandered through the swamps of Georgia, the dark pine forest of Wisconsin, the hardwood wilderness of Kentucky, or the rugged deserts of our Southwest and heard that scream pierce through the silence. Once one hears the scream of a bobcat, it is never forgotten. Some mistake the cry to be that of a mountain lion, but it is the bobcat's first line of defense. He hopes it will scare the hell out of a potential enemy, and it usually does.

That morning, though, all was tranquil and I felt ready to begin my daily routine. I had no idea that in a short while total pandemonium would engulf my home.

I entered the foyer, leaving the double front doors open behind me to let some fresh air into the living room.

Despite my precautions, my cough developed rapidly, dry at first, then deep in my chest. I pulled my inhaler from my pocket. It seemed to help a little with the first puff. Then I saw my wife washing dishes in the kitchen.

"Chi." I struggled to speak. "Call Teri in the office. Ask her to phone 911. I think I'm having an attack."

I forgot to preface that with "asthma," but it made no difference at that point. I fell to my knees, gasping for air between coughs, which were occurring more frequently.

"Teri!" I heard my wife yell into the two-way radio. "Your father is having an attack. Call 911!"

In three minutes Teri entered through the open doors and joined my wife at my side. "Lay all the way down, Dad," Teri instructed. "Is it your heart?"

"No . . . my lungs . . . asthma," I whispered.

"What can we do . . . get for you?" My wife's voice hinted at a bit of panic.

"Nothing," I answered. "The inhaler isn't doing its job."

The coughs continued. I felt as if someone was standing on my chest and choking my throat at the same time.

"I called 911," Teri assured. "Help is on the way. Herman is also phoning for help."

Herman can't clearly speak English, I thought. He often sounds like a German World War II officer when requesting something. I imagined him saying, "You will send help immediately! Do you understand? Jah?" But maybe, in view of my condition, that character quirk might help get results.

I closed my eyes for a moment, then felt something lightly brush my cheek. It was Trooper, pressing his nose and long whiskers against my face. His eyes were wide and his ears pointed directly at me. He sat back, but continued to stare at my face, trying to comprehend my problem and what to do about it.

"It's okay, Troop," I said as I reached to touch his side. There was no fooling the cat. He knew I was in trouble.

I heard an ambulance siren. It came closer and closer, then stopped and was replaced by an engine sound near the front porch.

What occurred during the next few minutes seemed at the time, and often since then, like a dream. I heard voices, but as breathing was difficult, I found it almost impossible to answer. Everything and everyone around me was moving in slow motion.

"Oh, thank God, they're here," Teri said with obvious relief.

"My husband can't breathe. It's his asthma!" Chi announced.

From that moment, and from my position flat on my back on the floor, the scene was foggy. My eyes strained to focus on the foyer.

Two paramedics had entered. One carried a large black bag slung over his shoulder.

At that moment, Trooper sprang from the floor, sailed over me, and landed on the coffee table. He sat erect, his fur bristling, and his mouth open in a snarl, as he exposed dangerous-looking teeth. Then Trooper began to growl, a low gurgling sound at first, but as the medics took their first step into the living room, the threat sounded ferocious. That quickly developed into an ear-piercing scream that tapered into another growl.

The medics froze, fearing to enter the room.

Trooper had never attacked a human before, perhaps simply because no one had provoked him. Actually, he had never bitten or scratched anyone but me, and that was when we were playing. In the past, Trooper often leaped to me and clamped his mouth down on my forearm. His powerful jaws squeezed just enough to prevent me from pulling away.

"Don't bite! Don't bite!" I would calmly order, and my wife or Teri or whoever was in the room at the time would yell "Don't bite Johnson! Trooper, don't bite Johnson!"

The cat thought this was all great fun and with eyes wide and wild looking would squeeze a little more, but always releasing his grip before breaking the skin. Then he would dash a short distance away, only to return and sit near me. I stroked his head each time, as his mother would have done, and complimented him with, "Good boy, Trooper. You are so strong." He seemed to crave the praise, but I never learned how he knew the amount of pressure to exert without destroying my arm. My only real skin damage came once when we were both new to the game. I made the mistake, a reflex reaction, of jerking my arm the moment he bit. The result was a torn shirt sleeve and some nasty scratches from his teeth. I couldn't blame the cat. I had to learn to trust him and not jerk as we played. Such is the value of trust among friends.

The paramedic's voice broke into my thoughts. "What kind of cat is that?"

"He's my dad's pet," Teri snapped, avoiding the question.

"Well, tell kitty to go play somewhere so we can do our work! Don't think he wants us near your dad."

"He doesn't like to be called 'kitty,'" Teri replied.

Trooper screamed again.

"OK! We won't call him kitty. Promise! Please ask him to move!"

At that same moment I heard the sound of another truck, only much louder this time. Suddenly two firemen, dressed in full firefighting uniforms, including black boots and helmets, stormed through the doorway and into the foyer. They were followed quickly

by two more firefighters and behind them a tall motorcycle policeman wearing a gold helmet. My foyer had become a little crowded.

From my prone position, the firemen appeared like something
from a 1950s science fiction movie, and I began to wonder how
many agencies Herman had called.

I am sure that to Trooper none of these intruders looked human; the odds, to the cat, no longer looked favorable. So Trooper
screamed once more, turned, and leaped fifteen feet to the bar's
countertop. There, in a crouched position, he resorted to a grumbling type of growl. Cats prefer heights and he had retreated to a
safer area.

The now brave medics were at my side. "You fellows need us?"
one of the firemen shouted from the foyer.

"Nope. Thanks. We're good."

The policeman moved aside and the firefighters returned to
their truck.

Teri went to Trooper and began to pet and comfort him. "It's
okay, Trooper," she was saying reassuringly, "they're going to help
Johnson."

Trooper's growl continued.

"Can you walk to the door with our help?" a medic asked me.
"We'll get you on a gurney at the ambulance."

"I can walk," I answered.

"That's a really big kitty," the policeman remarked as we
entered the foyer.

"He doesn't like to be called 'kitty,'" one of the medics responded with a smile.

The officer laughed and looked towards Teri. "What have you
been feeding kit . . . that cat? Wish mine was that big."

"Bad people," Teri joked.

"Well, he'll never go hungry in this town." The policeman
turned to the medics. You need an escort?"

"No thanks. We'll have this man at Saint Rose in a few
minutes. Not much traffic between here and there this time of day."

Teri and Chi were calling "Thank you," and as we went out the door, I paused to look back into the room. Chi was following, car keys and purse in hand.

"It's okay, Troop. These are friends. I'll be back soon!" I managed to say.

I didn't like the idea of returning to a hospital. It had been only two years since my surgery. But this time I was home in three days, breathing normally with new medicine, and I never suffered a similar attack again.

Trooper was waiting on the porch and brushed up against my leg the moment I stepped from the car. I had departed from this point and, to the cat, I would return to the same place. Chi informed me that he remained on the porch during those three days, leaving long enough to eat, then back at his "post," waiting.

Perhaps he felt uncomfortable in failing as a bodyguard. I hope not. He made an effort to protect me and frighten away those strange creatures who invaded our home. But the odds simply were too great. He had proven his devotion once more and we were together again, ready for another adventure.

CHAPTER 17

Little Brother

"One cat just leads to another."

Ernest Hemingway

"**D**OES HE BITE?" THE FEMALE UPS driver inquired as she entered our office with a large package.

Trooper was sitting on the table in the meeting room. I often forgot how big, and maybe dangerous, my cat could seem to first-time visitors.

The cat jumped to the floor and moved to rub against her leg in a friendly gesture.

"No," I answered. "He's never bitten anyone. He's shy around men, but sure likes women, as you can see. I think it has something to do with tone of voice."

"May I touch him?" she politely asked with a tone of sincere curiosity.

"Sure. He'll love it. He always loves female attention."

She reached down and scratched the top of the cat's head.

"I have a cat," she proudly announced. "He sleeps with me and never asks to borrow money."

"Good friend to have," I replied.

"This cat is sure fuzzy. Bet he'll be losing the winter coat soon."

"Oh, yes. My wife brushes him twice a day. He's shedding gobs of fur. His thinner summer coat is on the way because of this warm spring we're having."

"My cat gets fleas," she said. "Does this fellow get them too?"

"Funny you asked that," I answered. "No, he doesn't, and I don't know why. It's like his fur has something on it that fleas can't take."

"I think it's the creosote bushes he brushes against all day," Teri stated as she entered the room. "Looks like this package is for the shop, Dad."

In another minute the UPS driver was out the door and backing her noisy truck down the driveway.

Teri had presented an interesting theory about the creosote bush. The bush, with its waxy, small green leaves, dominates the Mojave Desert landscape below 4,000 feet elevation (Las Vegas sits about 2,100 feet above sea level). Trooper roamed among those bushes in our gully and in the desert around our ranch every day and night.

Creosote leaves are coated with a chemical resin, a sticky, wax-like substance which prevents water loss in our hot climate. It is this resin which emits a very peculiar odor, and that smell protects the plant from insects. Bugs simply don't like the smell, and neither do some people.

However, the plant was a blessing to the desert Native Americans who boiled the leaves in water to create a steam, which relieved congestion when inhaled. The mixture, or creosote, forms a tea which those people often use to alleviate stomach cramps and coughs.

Because of the plant's ability to survive with very little natural water and to repel insects, they often reach ages of over one hundred years, some more than a thousand years (based on carbon-14 tests).

I frequently noted a slight odor of creosote on Trooper's fur and have since concluded that this saved him from attacking fleas, ticks, and other insects.

I returned to my office and was about to place a phone call, when Teri went to the door and came back followed by a composed, middle-aged woman dressed in tight blue jeans and a bright yellow blouse, her dark hair, which hung loosely about her shoulders.

"Dad, this lady says she needs to speak with you." The look on my daughter's face revealed that the talk might not be pleasant.

"Yes, of course," I said, standing up to greet my visitor. "Will you have a seat?" I pointed to the empty chair across from my desk.

"No, thank you. I prefer to stand," she coldly answered.

"What may I do for you?"

"You are Mr. Johnson, correct?"

"Yes."

"Well"—she took a deep breath—"I've come to speak with you about your cat, your bobcat."

"What makes you think my cat is a bobcat?" I asked.

"A friend of mine lives near here. She said you are keeping a bobcat caged up at your home! I hope that is not true."

I studied the woman's face for a moment, then replied, "I have a cat and he is not in a cage or pen. Never has been. See for yourself. He's sleeping right over there in the chair." I pointed to the meeting room where Trooper remained asleep, apparently uninterested in the visitor.

"That is a bobcat!" she exclaimed, pointing at Trooper. "I moved here from the Bay Area. I've seen bobcats before in California!"

"So?"

"Where do you feed him?" she pushed, accusingly. "Where is his sand box? I suppose you lure him to your house every night."

I smiled. "He dines out a lot. His sand box? The entire Mojave Desert is his sand box," I added jokingly.

"Did you know it is unlawful to keep a bobcat?" she snapped, ignoring my humor.

"True in California. Laws are different in Nevada. This cat has been with me since 1987. The regulations regarding wildlife ownership were changed in 1994. I'm permitted to keep him because we were together before '94. Come"—I motioned with my hand—"let me show you something."

I moved to the large window above my desk. She followed, after a slight hesitation.

"Look out there," I said. "What do you see?"

"The desert," she replied.

"Exactly. That is where he goes whenever he wants. So he really is a free-range cat."

"Oh," she responded. "My friend told me that you keep the cat in a pen, that he gets loose now and then."

"Well, your information is wrong," I replied firmly.

Her eyes shifted, and she glanced about the room.

"You came here because you feel about something very strongly," I said. "I can only conclude you believe in saving wild animals, to let them remain wild and roam free."

"Yes." She spoke softly now. "I truly believe in doing what I can to protect our wild creatures."

"A wonderful endeavor. But your visit here was based on misinformation. It may come as a surprise to you, but I, too, am concerned about wildlife, in particular, wild cats. I wasn't always in that mode. Only since I met that cat in there. Now, if you want to help wild cats, you can try to prevent their slaughter."

"What are you talking about?"

"Do you know how many bobcats are caught in traps and killed in Nevada, or how many more are killed by hunters during hunting season, or how many are killed by poachers hunting out of season, without permits?"

"No, I don't."

"Over 3,000 are trapped for their fur each year. A pelt can bring up to $600 from buyers in China or Russia. Another 1,000 wild cats are shot by hunters or poachers in Nevada alone. That's a slaughter!"

"That is horrible," she sighed.

"I believe people should be allowed to hunt, with a permit and in a season. But the season should be shorter and there must be a limit set on the number of cats killed."

"We should save them," she replied definitively, "but let them remain in the wild."

Then, with a nod of her head, she started towards the door, turned, and added, "I'll think about your point, Mr. Johnson."

And she was gone.

I sat down at my desk with a sigh of relief at her departure.

Teri reentered the office, having politely remained in the meeting room during the confrontation.

"Want a cup of coffee, Dad?" she asked.

"No. No, thanks."

"Think she'll return?"

"I hope not," I answered. "She has some serious frustrations and I guess I appeared as an easy target. Let's hope the rest of the day is less eventful."

I got up and walked into the meeting room. Trooper had remained asleep during the encounter. I sat in the chair next to him. Watching a cat sleep can bring peace to a troubled mind.

He let out a soft cry and his legs twitched. I knew he was dreaming, and I concluded it must be a troubling one. I reached to touch his back in hopes of breaking the dream's direction.

The old expression "let sleeping dogs lie" doesn't have to be restricted to canines; it can also apply to cats. There is a danger in waking an animal, as he may respond violently if the mind is still occupied with the dream. That fast response could result in a bite or scratch before he realizes he is awake and free of the dream, and there is nothing to fear.

I nudged him again, withdrawing my hand quickly. He didn't snap into action. Instead, his eyes opened and he stared ahead.

"You were having a bad dream," I said to the cat.

His sleepy eyes shifted to me.

"What were you dreaming about?" I questioned.

He stretched, arching his back, and lay down on his side, eyes locked on me the whole time. I scratched the top of his head between the ears, the spot where no cat can reach with a paw.

What pictures does the cat brain create from dark corners? Does he relive the moment his family was killed by coyotes, or me finding him? Or would his nightmare be of hunger or fear of rejection, that I might leave and never return, or of growing old without love?

I, too, worried about coyotes, as did everyone in our area. I wanted to tell the cat never to stand and fight. There would be no chance for survival against a pack of those terrorists. He should run and jump or climb to a high place, a wall, car roof, or tree. But suppose he couldn't reach those high places of safety? He couldn't outrun a coyote. So there, perhaps, I had his bad dream. It was also mine.

He had fallen asleep again, a peaceful sleep this time, with nice dreams, the way dreams should always be.

"Dad!"

Teri's call startled me.

"Yes?"

"A nurse at Doctor Marg's office just called. There's good news."

"What?"

"There's a couple who would like to adopt the black cats. Wanted to know if we still have them. I told them, yes. She wants you to call her back, pronto!"

I phoned the nurse, and was given the contact number for the interested couple. They had lost a pair of cats over the past two years, so this pair seemed perfect. I was excited about the adoption. We had given the girls a home away from the dangers of the desert, but there were so many restrictions that had been placed by Trooper and enforced by myself. They would never be completely comfortable. I was certain they had once been "inside" cats and that's what these new owners were prepared to offer.

Doctor Marg recommended and approved the couple. I could ask for no more.

A few days later, the couple arrived and were very pleasant. To my surprise, the two cats came to us while we stood talking in the driveway. And when the wife reached down to touch Mama, the cat thankfully did not back away. In fact, both cats greeted their new humans with purrs and leg rubs.

I glanced towards the office. Sitting in the doorway, Trooper studied the transaction with no obvious emotion. I wondered how he felt about the girls' departure. Would he be sad or relieved?

"Now they'll have a good home," Chi said to the couple. "A better life."

Again, another surprise. The lady picked up each cat and placed them in the back seat of her car with no difficulty. We waved goodbye as they drove out the driveway. And then they were gone.

It all happened so fast. I wondered if the girls understood that they were on the way to a good home and a good life.

Sometimes change can happen fast and goodbyes never last long enough. I would not forget those kitties, how they led me to Trooper when he was trapped, or the look of gratitude and hope in their eyes when we first welcomed them to our yard. Had they given up while waiting in that culvert, blocked by a big cat, the same cat who later permitted them into the house so they could be warm and safe during a very cold night.

Trooper moved from the doorway. I wanted desperately to know what he was thinking. I was certain he had feelings about the departure of the girls.

Three or four days after the black cats' relocation, Herman reported that Trooper was using the culvert pipe to pass under the narrow country road that ran along the front of our property and continued on another mile to a main highway. The cat believed he needed to investigate something on the west side of the road

"Why?" I asked the German. "Something special over there?" Herman confessed he didn't know.

We soon had the answer. I was standing in the office at the file cabinet when Herman's voice came through the two-way radio.

"There's a gold baby cat coming with Trooper."

"What the hell is he talking about?" I said, looking at Teri.

"You know Herman," she replied. "Just as Jim is the self-appointed newsman for the neighborhood, Herman elected himself special investigator and reporter for your property. He believes he's competing with Trooper for the job."

"What gold cat?" I spoke into the radio.

No answer.

I walked to the door and discovered that Herman spoke the truth. Before my eyes was a cat parade. Trooper strutted proudly by as if he had just captured something. Behind him, running to catch up, was a small golden tabby with chest and paws of snow-white fur.

Trooper sat down and looked over his shoulder as the cat, a little larger than a kitten, reached his side. Trooper tilted his head down and the small one rubbed against it. It was an odd sight. The tabby was less than a quarter of the size of Trooper.

"Troop, where did you find your friend?"

He looked at me a moment and then continued up the center of the driveway, moving towards the kitchen entrance. Once again, the gold cat struggled to keep up.

"Where did Trooper find that kitten?" Teri asked as she joined my side.

"I don't know," I answered. "I didn't see anyone down at the road."

"He's a cute little cat," she said. "Must belong to someone in the area."

"Yeah. Unless someone dropped it off."

"You mean, like the black cats?"

"I hope not. We'll ask around. That cat couldn't have traveled far. He's too young."

"Johnson! Please come to the kitchen!" came my wife's voice broke through on the radio. "Yellow kitten in here with Trooper!"

"Seems we have a Trooper tracking system!" Teri joked.

I radioed back to Chi, "What are the cats doing?"

"Yellow cat is eating Trooper's food." she answered.

"What's Trooper doing?"

"He's just sitting and watching yellow cat eat."

Teri and I glanced at one another for a second without speaking. We both surely had questions but there was no time to discuss them.

It was time for me to investigate. I quickly reached the kitchen to find Chi standing and watching the gold cat, who was enjoying a snack of dry food.

"Kitten must be very important," she said. "Trooper is letting him eat his food!"

"Must be. Trooper brought him all the way up here to feed him."

"He is so cute. Big eyes. Lots of expression. Where did yellow cat come from?" she asked, puzzled.

"No idea. Trooper must have found him somewhere in the desert."

Trooper moved into the living room, followed by the tabby. It seemed that Trooper was going to introduce his new friend to his favorite couch. Trooper jumped on the couch and curled up in the corner.

The yellow cat began to meow and attempted to join Trooper, but he was unable to reach that height. He tried again, and toppled backward. Finally he gave up and fell asleep next to the couch.

"What do we do now?" Chi asked. "Two black cats leave, so your cat brings home a gold baby!"

"Well, for now, let's let them rest. Trooper has been treating that kitten like he was his little brother. But they sure look different."

"That's what I'll call him," Chi said.

"What?"

"Let's call him Little Brother, until we find his owner."

"And if there is no owner to be found?"

"Then . . . we'll let Trooper decide if he can stay."

"I think Trooper has already made that decision."

CHAPTER 18

Mystery Solved

"I have studied philosophers and many cats. The wisdom of cats is infinitely superior."

Hippolyte Taire

"LOOK AT THOSE FUNNY CATS," Teri said as she stood at the office window. Her attention was focused on something a dozen or so feet away in the desert.

I joined her and began to laugh.

"Oh, Trooper is introducing Little Brother to a cactus flower. That's all," I said.

"They've been at that cactus for a few minutes," she noted. "I first thought they had some animal spotted in there. Now I see it's the flowers that have their attention. Those beautiful magenta blossoms must have attracted Trooper. Is the cactus a beaver tail or prickly pear?"

"Hard to tell from here. The beaver tail is a type of prickly pear. So, either name is correct, I guess."

"Look at Trooper," she said, pointing. "He pushes his nose into the blossom, then backs off and opens his mouth. Brother starts to do the same, but his mouth doesn't open. What's that all about?"

"Trooper usually does it when smelling something. He even tests the wind that way. He smells with his nose and opens his mouth to smell again. Looks like Brother hasn't learned that yet."

"What?"

"Cats have an organ in the roof of the mouth that helps them identify and record things by smell."

"Can we do that?" she asked with a sly smile.

"Well, maybe when humans were first evolving, long ago. Cats can test a smell carried by the wind and determine if an animal is prey or predator, if a cat is a male or female."

"They're sure making a big issue of flower smelling," she said. "Look at the cactus on the other side of the gulley. How beautiful! They have yellow blossoms."

"I think Trooper is teaching Brother not only how to use the art of smelling, but how to avoid the spines . . . the needles. I'm sure he's learned through trial and error how to avoid the needles while enjoying the sweet smell of the flower. You know, that cactus has been a staple of Mexican and Central American people for thousands of years."

"You're kidding!"

"I'm serious. The oval pods can be prepared and eaten like a vegetable. But one has to take care to remove all the needle-like spines. There are two types. That's what Trooper is showing Brother. The petals of the flower are often eaten as a salad, and its pear like a fruit. You've seen cactus candy for sale in gift shops?"

"Yes. Here, and in Arizona."

"Most come from the prickly pear."

"Do wild cats eat the flower pods?" she asked with genuine curiosity.

"I don't think so. Some animals do, but the cat will wait for meat."

"Look!" said Teri, once again pointing. "The cactus lesson must be over. They are heading this way, side by side. Trooper has been showing Brother every piece of furniture in this office."

"That comes as no surprise. I'm sure enjoying watching Trooper play like a kitten again. This game of chasing and rolling about reminds me of his early days. I guess we all enjoy being a kid again, once in a while."

Brother, of course, like children, was a bundle of pure energy. He moved about like a windup toy until collapsing for a nap. While playing together, if Trooper became tired, or for whatever reason lost interest, he held the little cat down with his paw for a few moments to subdue him, and then simply walked away.

The activities and explorations for the two continued for two weeks, and still, we had no idea just where Brother had come from. There had been no "lost cat" posters in the neighborhood, no listing in the paper's lost-and-found section, and local animal hospitals reported they had no one looking for a lost gold cat.

So we were left with our original conclusion: Trooper found him at a nearby ranch, or someone dropped him off along the road to dispose of him.

We became, each day, more attached to the little cat, especially since Trooper not only accepted him, but had begun an education program. The big cat had assumed the position of both mother and father, and thus far appeared to be enjoying the responsibility. But we had yet to learn the true personality of the little cat. That would soon be revealed as he began to grow.

On morning about two weeks after Brother's arrival, the mystery of his origin was officially solved.

The whirring sound of an electric golf cart announced the arrival of Jim Butler. Then silence as the cart came to a halt in the driveway near my office door. In a moment the towering figure of Jim entered the office.

"This place got any coffee?" he inquired with typical swagger and a healthy grin.

"Sure, Jim. Black, or lots of cream and sugar?" I shot back as a joke. I already knew the answer.

"What! Do you think I'm a sissy sailor? Black, of course!"

"Sit down, Jim. Tell me what brings you here, while Teri gets you a cup."

"Well." He paused. "How's my cat doing?"

Teri and I exchanged a quick glance.

"I didn't know you had any pets," I said. "What color is your cat?"

"Was my cat," he replied, smiling. Then he continued after taking a long sip of coffee.

"He was gold. Antique gold. Your bobcat kidnapped him. Led him over here."

"Well." I hesitated. "Trooper brought home a gold cat about two weeks ago. We have been trying to find his owner ever since. I guess, now, we've found him. Why did you wait so long to tell us, if you knew he was over here?"

"I wanted to see if he would come back on his own. I hoped he decided to stay over here. I'm not a cat person, though, and I knew you guys could take good care of him."

"He's doing fine," I assured him, "playing with Trooper all the time. Would you like to see him, Jim?"

"No, thank you. Not necessary. I know he's okay and that makes me feel good. He wasn't mine, anyway. I just felt sorry for the little fellow so I set out some food and water for him every day."

"He wasn't your pet? Just a stray?"

"No. Not a pet. It's a sad story. Makes me sick to think about it. I reacted too slow . . ."

"Does he have his shots yet?" Teri asked.

"No shots. In fact, I never even touched him. Just fed him. So please keep him . . . as my gift."

I breathed a deep sigh of relief. Apparently Little Brother now belonged to us, or at least to Trooper.

"More coffee, Jim?" Teri inquired.

"Yeah. Thank you. I never tasted coffee until I joined the Navy. Now I can't stop drinking the stuff."

"Better coffee than whiskey," I said.

"True. And I never tasted whiskey until the Navy, either. I wasn't even of age the first time I tried it."

I circled back: "In regards to the cat, Jim. You said you reacted too slowly. What way?" I was puzzled.

"Have you named that cat yet?" he asked, as if to avoid an answer. "I never gave him a name."

"Yes. Chiaki named him Little Brother for the way he follows Trooper around."

Jim rubbed his right knee with his hand and inhaled a long breath, releasing it slowly.

"I'll tell you about . . . Brother, if you really want to know."

"Of course we do," said Teri. "We're curious."

"About eight weeks ago," Jim began with a clear voice, "a tan-colored mother cat decided to deliver her kittens at the bottom of my back porch steps. As best I could tell, she had four kittens. She kept them in the crawl space under my house, which has just enough clearance for the family to go in and out."

"Any idea where she came from?" Teri asked.

"Nope. She simply showed up, as cats will sometimes do."

"And?" I pushed.

"And," Jim continued. "They were doing okay for the first three weeks. Then, one night, the predators struck."

"The coyotes."

"Oh!"

"I heard a cat scream," Jim continued, his body leaning forward. "I was watching TV and went to open the back door. Coyotes, four of them! They had already killed mother cat. One was carrying her away. I went to get my gun. But in that minute or two, by the time I got to the back porch, they were gone, and so were the kittens. The brutes had attacked, killed, and retreated, all in less than three minutes!"

Jim paused to take another sip of coffee, then set the cup down at the edge of my desk.

"Sometimes," he said, "I wish I had never stopped smoking. That scene made me nervous and sick to my stomach. The next morning I went out, right at dawn, to see if any kittens escaped the massacre. Sure enough, I heard a kitten crying. I pulled him out from the crawl space. Gave him some tuna fish and water and meat scraps each day. That yellow cat ate real good. Poor guy. He didn't appear to have any wounds on his skin so he must have crawled under the house to safety when the battle . . . no! It weren't no battle! It was a massacre!"

As Jim spoke, my thoughts flashed to the day I found Trooper. How similar their early experience.

"So what happened next?" Teri's voice broke a moment of silence.

"I told the gold cat to hide under the house, which he did each night. During the mornings he came out and I watched him play about the yard. My rifle was always ready. I wanted the thugs to return, but they haven't. But guess who did show up!"

"Who?" I asked, fully expecting him to say it was an old Navy buddy.

"Your big cat," came the quick answer. "They began to play together and took naps, side-by-side in the tree shade. It seemed your cat had assumed the position of bodyguard. When your cat walked away the gold cat meowed a few times, then went to sleep. But then about two weeks ago, I guess, they both felt the kitten was strong enough to follow the big cat. I watched as the kitten followed Trooper across the road and into your front yard. I waited these days to see if he might return. He didn't, so I figured he's happy here."

"You know we'll take good care of him," Teri said.

"I'm sure you all will. By the way, Johnson, you know why older cats sometimes adopt a younger cat, don't you?"

"No," I replied, "not really. But if this is another one of your Navy stories, I'll ask Teri to step out for a while."

Jim chuckled, "Got nothing to do with Navy days. No, it's an old saying, sort of a belief in some circles. Older cats adopt a younger cat because the older one knows he don't have much longer to live. He wants to be sure that his human friend always has a cat companion."

His story gave me an uncomfortable feeling in the pit of my stomach. I knew Trooper was aging, but thought little of it because he always seemed so active. And, like most people, I hold onto the naïve belief that our loved ones live forever.

"One thing about you, Jim," I finally said, "you always bring a dab of depressing news mixed with the good stuff!"

Jim replied with a laugh, "But that's the way life goes, isn't it?"

"Yeah. I suppose so."

Then Jim decided, wisely, to change the subject.

"Do you know the Packer family? They have a small ranch about a mile and a half southeast of here."

"No," I responded, "I don't think I've met them."

"Well . . . Mrs. Packer, Ruth is her name, says she knows you, or at least knows your cat."

"Trooper visits that far away?" I said, puzzled. "He didn't cause any problems, did he?"

"No. None. But Ruth did have a few interesting things to report the other day. Seems they invested in a flock of African guinea hens, about fifty I think she said."

"What kind of bird is that?" Teri asked. "They're not natural to this desert, are they?"

"Not at all. The Packers want to see if the birds will survive around here. It's more of a fun project for them than anything else. They are funny-looking birds, all gray feathers and a long neck, topped with a head that looks like a vulture. They are about the size of a fat chicken. Ruth is fascinated with the birds for some reason, and thinks of them as pets, not food. The problem is, those birds wander about in groups, often traveling a mile before returning home. They visited my place. I call them 'the long-range patrol.'"

"What's this got to do with Trooper? Did he kill one of her birds?" I asked.

"Well, no. But this is where the story gets interesting. Ruth had seen your cat before, so when he showed up to check the birds, she naturally worried he would make a meal out of them. He didn't. He just sat back and watched them. They make a lot of chatter as they move about, so that surely got Trooper's attention. But you can guess who has been making a meal out of the birds!"

"Coyotes!" Teri and I spoke together, with disgust.

"Right! Of course! Now, here comes a real shocker. Ruth reports that your cat was up in a cottonwood tree in her yard. From separate positions, Ruth and Trooper watched as the coyotes rushed in and snatched a few of her birds. Then, a day or two later, she reported the same scene. Trooper observed the coyote attack from the tree. Apparently those animals were so busy picking off birds they never noticed the cat above them."

"Why the hell would my cat travel so far, two times, to watch coyotes kill birds?" I asked.

"Don't you get it?" Jim snapped with a broad grin. "You've been with that cat for years. You should know his thinking. He is one very smart kitty. All wild cats are, by nature. He's planning something, I'm sure of it."

I looked at Teri. Her face was etched with a puzzling frown.

"OK, Jim, I give up. Spell it out for us! Share a sample of your vast wildlife knowledge," I said with a grin.

"The birds are educational bait," said Jim with a slight laugh.

"Bait?"

"Yeah, bait. Ruth, her husband, and I discussed it. Of course, they are angry about losing their birds. Trying to raise them in the desert with coyotes around was . . . between you and me, a bad idea to begin with."

"My cat, Jim. Let's get back to him. Why does my cat return to the tree and watch the killing? You think he is just curious?"

"Tactics, my friend. Your cat is smart. He is observing, no, studying the tactics of those coyotes. He's learning their attack system, their killing methods, order of rank, their speed, and which one is the leader, the strongest. The coyotes know those ugly birds can fly and run fast, so their attack must be swift, else the birds will escape into a tree. Your cat knows exactly the behavior of the coyote when it moves in for the kill."

"That's an interesting theory," I said.

"Of course it is. And the Packers agree. The cat has his plans and he surely is not going to go after a pack of coyotes. Maybe he'll find a chance to take them one at a time."

I stared at the floor, thinking of Jim's report. Trooper might have been gathering "field intelligence," as we call it in the army. And I remembered something Dr. Marg once said, to the effect that "cats are superior observers." But, as I have learned, they don't always take action with what they learned.

"When did all this take place, Jim?"

"About a week after the coyotes killed the cats in my yard. Then, in a few days, I noticed Trooper visiting. Maybe Trooper brought the kitten over here thinking you and him, together, could protect him."

Then, as if on cue, Trooper walked in, followed by Little Brother. They paused and looked at us. Brother started towards Jim and gave a few meows.

"He sure knows you, Jim. You want him back?"

"No, thank you," Jim replied. "He's a cute little cat, but he'll be much happier here with you guys. I'm not much with pets."

Trooper moved to the meeting room and jumped into a chair. Brother made an attempt to join him, but failed with his first leap. On the second try he succeeded by sinking his claws into the seat cushion and pulled himself up as his back legs kicked at the air. Trooper licked at Brother's head for a brief cleaning, then they curled up and fell asleep.

CHAPTER 19
The Legend of Fat Face

"There are two means of refuge from the miseries of life: music and cats."

Dr. Albert Schweitzer

THE TIME HAD COME TO take Brother to Dr. Marg for his vaccinations and surgery, to be "fixed" or neutered. Luckily, it was also time for Trooper's annual vaccinations.

For most cat owners, a doctor's visit isn't a major event, and almost certainly not a challenging one. But after years of experience transporting my big cat, I always expected a struggle, though I must admit, Trooper had mellowed somewhat in his senior years.

But Chi and I didn't know what to expect from Brother. He was a cuddly kind of cat, and when we first introduced him to his new crate he hopped in and out, probably believing it was part of a game we had planned. We even entertained the thought of Chi simply holding him until we arrived at the clinic. We soon concluded, though, that was a bad idea. If Brother were to leap from her arms, not only might we never find him again, he could get seriously hurt. The travel crate is always the best when moving

159

an animal, big or small. With Trooper there had never been any choice. He was simply too big and feisty for any way but the crate.

So plan A was to take both cats to the vet in a single trip. But when I phoned for an appointment, a receptionist suggested we try a new program they had implemented.

"Doctor Marg is getting ready to retire," the young voice informed me, "and her new partner, Doctor Shelmacker, suggested you may wish to consider our mobile clinic." She explained that Trooper could receive his shots at our home, and then Brother could be transported to the hospital separately for his surgery. I agreed, as it sounded interesting in theory and was certainly easier than crating Trooper.

The mobile clinic arrived late morning the next day, driven by a professional animal paramedic, with two nurses as passengers. I had never seen any of the trio before, and at that moment should have known we would have a problem.

The nurses stated they had reviewed Trooper's file, knew about his origin, size, medical history, and were thus anxious to meet him. Their enthusiasm unfortunately was not to be shared by the cats, who were asleep on the living room couch when the nurses entered the foyer.

Trooper awoke like the snap of a twig. His nose twitched as he stared at the two young ladies in their crisp white uniforms. Though usually interested in females, something told him this visit was different. He jumped to the floor, followed by Brother, and they trotted to the guest bedroom. Trooper took a position on top of the bed, facing the door, while Brother scooted underneath.

"Perhaps I can pull the little yellow cat out," one nurse said. "We shouldn't bother the big one."

Her statement was greeted by a heavy growl from Trooper.

I knew he would not attack the nurse. He was bluffing as a warning, partly to protect Brother, but mostly to encourage the nurses to leave, which they did.

Though the idea of a mobile clinic was a good one in theory, it wouldn't work for Trooper. So we were left with plan A and struggled with the big cat to push him into his crate. We gently lifted Brother into his with no difficulty.

In a few days the entirety of the trip—shots, the insertion of Brother's computer locator chip, and his surgery—was, at least for us, a fading memory and the two cats were back to exploring their outside world.

One afternoon Las Vegas was treated to a rare heavy rainstorm, which lasted almost an hour. But quickly, the sun was out again, and with its heat began to boil the moisture from the desert floor, producing a fog-like mist that drifted lazily over the landscape. But several puddles of water remained in our driveway, which, for Brother, who had never seen such a thing, presented something that warranted investigation. As expected, he withdrew his paw after a slight touch of the water. Then, to our surprise, Trooper waded through a four-inch-deep puddle, perhaps to show the little cat there was nothing to fear.

Indeed, it was a strange move for the big cat. At our first home, Trooper never even entered the fish pond, resisting the temptation while watching the fish swim about. As with most cats, a touch of the water with his paw was enough, though he did smack the water to encourage the fish to entertain him.

Bobcats are known to be excellent swimmers when raised in an area where small bodies of water flow. While they do not engage in recreational swimming as many breeds of dogs enjoy, they do swim to cross from one side of a body to another for whatever reason. Of course, desert bobcats very rarely have the opportunity to test their swimming ability. Creek and river beds remain dry most of the year, except when enough rain produces flash floods, and a glance at fast-moving water, carrying debris, is enough to discourage any attempt to enter.

Brother moved back and forth with nervous energy at the puddle's edge, trying to get the nerve to follow Trooper, but he soon gave up, resorting to simply testing the water with a paw.

That evening I received a phone call from Ruth Packer, the women with the African guinea hens. Jim had recently related their problem with coyotes. After a brief exchange of pleasantries, I stated, "I'm sorry to learn about the loss of your birds."

"Thank you. We still have about thirty, although they are difficult to count. They travel a bit."

"Yes, Jim told me."

"Well, we got revenge on those coyotes. My husband managed to shoot one with his rifle yesterday, just about dusk. There are still three in the pack, but they are staying clear of us for a while."

"I'm so glad your husband shot one," I said.

"Have my birds been to visit your place? I hope they don't cause trouble with all the noise they make."

"No. They haven't been over here yet. And I'm sure they'll be of no problem for us. Again, thank your husband. Those coyotes have really created a reign of terror around here for years."

"Your beautiful cat has been patrolling our ranch from time to time. We thought he was wild at first, but then Jim told us he is your pet. We were surprised he didn't kill one of our birds, but he has never bothered them. He just sits and watches."

"I'm sure happy he hasn't harmed your birds," I said. "But please let me know at once if he causes any alarm."

"He's been studying the coyotes from our tree. Do you think he plans to attack them?"

"I don't think he'll attack the coyotes," I replied, "unless they get him cornered, which, of course, I hope that never happens."

"Well," said Ruth, "other than calling to introduce myself, I really wanted to tell you about Fat Face. No doubt he'll be visiting you."

"Who?"

"Fat Face! He's a great big tom cat, almost the size of your cat. He steals our cat's food we put out on the porch and growls and hisses if we try to get near him. My husband calls him Fat Face because his head is so very large, as is his face, which is all scarred from fights long ago, I guess. My husband says he looks like a cat from hell!"

"Very strange. Where did he come from, other than hell?" I chuckled with the thought.

"No one knows. He's just a rōnin."

"A what?"

"Rōnin. You know, a Japanese warrior who wanders around. Fat Face fights with other cats near here and steals their food too. I thought I should warn you about Fat Face. Jim says you have a young cat. I hope Fat Face doesn't hurt him!"

I thanked Ruth for her warning and agreed our families should "get acquainted someday soon."

"Chi!" I called to my wife, who was in another room.

"What is it?"

"Tell me about rōnin!"

"Ramen noodles?"

"No! Rōnin, not ramen!"

"Don't shout!" she said, entering the room. "Are you asking about Japanese rōnin?"

"Yes. What does it mean if someone says a cat is a rōnin? Means he wanders about, right?"

"Kind of so," she replied, "Rōnin means 'wave man'. They move about like waves on ocean."

"Why do they move about? Looking for food?"

"Maybe," she replied, "not always. A real rōnin was once a samurai, a warrior who followed the code of bushido and had a master to serve and protect."

"The way of the warrior code," I interjected.

"Correct. If samurai's master is killed or dies, samurai has no job and moves about doing odd jobs, unless some new master hires him."

"And if he doesn't find a job, then what?"

"He may kill himself by ritual seppuku to save honor, of course!"

"Ugh! Not good to be unemployed. I doubt that a cat will commit seppuku."

"Cat? What are you talking about?"

I explained my conversation with Ruth and her use of the word rōnin. Now I was curious to see this Fat Face feline. Could he be so horrible?

My most immediate problem was our sleeping arrangement. Since the beginning of our relationship, Trooper had found comfort by curling up under my right arm at night and falling asleep. Usually after I fell asleep, he got up and ventured outside. The time of his return was unpredictable, but I could count on him to be at my side, or on my chest, to wake me in the morning.

Chiaki called him "my fuzzy alarm clock." We could count on his punctuality. If I awoke at 6 a.m. two days in a row, Trooper would be there a few minutes before 6 on the third morning. If I decided to sleep late and awoke at 9 a.m., the second morning Trooper would be there a few minutes before 9.

In later years, I had a theory as to reasons the cat joined me to fall asleep and then left after he was certain I was, indeed, asleep and not pretending. In a way, it reminds me of a human mother putting her child asleep and then checking on him from time to time.

So, for years, this sleeping arrangement worked for my cat, my wife, and I. Now, with Little Brother, the situation became difficult. Within a few weeks Little Brother was strong enough to leap into bed with us. Of course, as a good "copy cat," as well as being extremely affectionate, he wanted to join Trooper and snuggle under my right arm. And that is where cat friendship, Brother or no Brother, ended. I belonged to Trooper and he was not about to share me.

To prevent Brother from joining us, Trooper would give a low growl. Brother backed off, crying or whimpering as he lay at my feet. He continued to cry until he fell asleep. After a few days of frustration (and sadness for Brother), the situation was solved with a compromise.

After a number of tries, Brother discovered he could snuggle under my left arm with no objection from Trooper. So there I was, both arms around cats who fell asleep before I did. I considered myself, though somewhat uncomfortable, to be very fortunate to have the love of two fuzzy animals.

But soon I found a solution to this new situation. I pretended to snore, faking sleep, and within three or four minutes, Trooper jumped to the floor, followed by Brother, and they were off to a night's adventure.

Shortly after the sleeping arrangement problem was settled, Chi and I were having breakfast in the kitchen when a cat scream startled us. I knew by the pitch and volume of the sound that it did not come from Trooper.

"Is that Little Brother yelling?" Chi asked.

"I don't think so."

Then a loud series of yowling and growling came from a very angry cat threatening something. That was quickly followed by a number of soft sounding meows.

"We had better see what's going on in the backyard," I said as I opened the kitchen door.

The yowling continued as I stepped onto the stoop in the bright morning sun.

There before me, perhaps twenty feet away, stood the ugliest large cat I had ever seen.

His long skinny tail hung as if it had been broken in two places and his gray fur was so thin that old battle scars were clearly visible on his body and neck. Half of one ear was missing, the wound having healed long ago, and his massive head, also pocked with scars, held a wide, flat face. His threatening appearance was accentuated by deep yowls and growls the likes of which I had never heard. In fact, they sounded almost as loud as Trooper's.

Fat Face had arrived! Because of the cat's odd and mangled appearance, there could be no doubting his identity.

What had the cat so angry was the fact that his advance was being blocked by our first line of defense, which surprisingly was neither Herman nor Trooper, but Little Brother.

The tiny gold cat stood his ground ten feet away from his giant opponent. The fur on Brother's ringed tail had bristled and his ears lay flat, back against his small head. He was prepared for battle by instinct only, as he had no previous experience in fighting.

For every horrible sound issued by Fat Face, Brother replied with a pitiful meow. When Fat Face elevated the volume of his growls, Brother answered with two faint meows. And then, to my amazement, Brother advanced his challenge by moving three feet closer to his enemy.

"Do something," Chi urged as she joined me on the stoop. "That big animal is going to make cat burger out of Little Brother!"

"I'm not sure what . . ." I started to say when a brown blur of fur rushed in on the scene with terrific speed. Trooper had come to the rescue. In an instant he positioned himself at Brother's right side and, without making a sound, scooped up the little cat and sent him tumbling in our direction. He then confronted Fat Face with a prolonged, guttural growl.

But Brother refused to be forced out of the action and rushed back to Trooper's side. This time Trooper growled sharply at him. Brother responded with a series of meows only to be tossed out of the way by a swing of Trooper's front leg and large paw, which appeared to actually scoop the little cat from the ground. It was as if Trooper told him, "Stay out of this. You're too young."

Brother's pride was crushed. With big sad eyes he scrambled up the steps, meowing at me, and then pressed his body against my leg. I leaned down and stroked his back, consoling him with praise.

"You're such a brave kitty," I told him. "You saved us from that mean old cat."

Brother began to purr and sat down next to me to watch the pending duel.

Trooper did not scream in response to all the racket created by Fat Face. Instead, he responded with growls and snarls, which, knowing my cat, sounded somewhat restrained.

Fat Face was, indeed, almost the size of Trooper, and judging from his scars, he never backed away from a fight.

Suddenly Fat Face sprang forward, aiming for Trooper's neck. Trooper moved sideways, grabbing the attacker and slamming him to the ground. He held Fat Face down and prepared to deliver a deadly bite.

Anyone who has witnessed a cat fight between two males knows that the speed of action can only be measured in split seconds. Every movement is lightning fast and it is almost impossible to judge which cat did what.

This fight seemed to end as fast as it began. Fat Face was stupidly brave, but not ready to die. He stopped kicking and lay still. Trooper leaped backward into an attack position, waiting for the big gray cat to make a threatening move.

But Fat Face apparently had enough. From where I stood I could see no fresh cuts on either cat. Fat Face began to slink away, holding his odd-looking tail down. Then he paused at about twenty feet and went into a crouched position. Was he planning another attack?

Trooper rolled over on his back, exposing his belly, and snapped a few quick glances at his enemy as if to say, "come on back. I dare you."

I knew Trooper's trick. He had used that trap so many times while we were playing. A movement at his belly resulted in my arm being grabbed by his mouth, while front legs wrapped around and held me in place. At the same instant, both rear legs kicked simultaneously. For us it was a game, and he never extended his claws. Yet an enemy falling for the trick would be shredded by the rear paws, while powerful legs held him firm.

But Fat Face was an experienced warrior, not about to be lured into that trap. He stood up and walked slowly to the gully, making a strange grumbling sound as he disappeared into the brush.

Trooper sat up and froze in position until certain the enemy had left the battlefield. Then he walked towards the front yard, heading to the office. Brave Little Brother jumped from the stoop and raced to catch up with his friend. Trooper paused as he reached his side and leaned down so they could touch heads. They continued on together at a slow pace.

I believe Trooper had no intention of harming that ugly cat. He was simply giving him a mild warning: "Don't come here!"

The big event was over. Little Brother proved himself foolish, but brave, and also very sensitive. But I had a feeling we had not seen the last of Fat Face.

CHAPTER 20
Peace Is Shattered

"A cat's eyes are windows enabling us to see into another world."

Old Irish Legend

SOME SAY THAT CATS ONLY meow at people, not other felines, but that is not true. Cats will meow at other cats for a variety of reasons. Brother facing down Fat Face is a perfect example of this. Of course, Brother had not yet mastered the art of growling, yowling, or screaming. He only knew how to meow. A cat's meow to another feline may, at first, sound similar to the ones he issues to people, but the feelings behind the meowing are different. To use an analogy: my wife often smiles at me, and at other people. The smile to me has a different meaning than it does to others, and this is because of feelings. Indeed, the same is true with cats. A "cat's meow" means different things to different people, other cats, and objects.

A friend of mine, preparing to move out of state, gave me his cuckoo clock, which I hung about five feet from the floor in our dining room. I had always been fascinated with the engineering of those clocks, and was pleased that this one kept excellent time. It had been designed so the little cuckoo bird only sprang from hiding on the hour and half hour, which was fine with me, because after the first day, the *cuckoo* sound, with the birds appearing, became a little annoying, especially at night.

The clock gained a true admirer the next day.

"Oh how cute!" Chiaki exclaimed when she entered the room to find Trooper sitting in an alert position beneath the clock. Next to him lay Brother, who greeted the cuckoo bird with a tender meow each time it sprang forward.

Over the next day and a half, I noticed that Trooper had somehow estimated the arrival of the bird. Of course, cats can't tell time the way that humans do, but I was reminded of one old question which haunted me: How did the cat know the hour I awoke? Now, however he managed it, Trooper succeeded in calculating the arrival of the bird. We watched from the living room as Trooper, followed by Brother, arrived a few minutes before the hour and waited.

It was 11 a.m. The cuckoo would appear and make its sound eleven times; just the amount of time the cat needed.

Before we could shout or respond in any way, Trooper jumped, snatched the toy bird with his mouth, and ripped it free of its mechanism.

Landing on all four feet, he placed his prize on the carpet for Brother to smell. The little cat meowed at the bird, picked it up, and the two trotted outside through their door in the kitchen.

"You knew that was going to happen," Chi said, with a slightly scolding tone.

"Well." I smiled. "I didn't think he would actually catch the bird. I thought he was content to just watch it."

"Sure, sure," she replied, not quite believing me. "But your cat is teaching that young one bad habits."

As for the clock, it continued to cuckoo on the hour, but without the bird, until I removed it from the wall and placed it in a closet.

Shortly after the cuckoo bird attack, I strolled outside expecting to find the cats somewhere along my way to the office

I entered the office, passing the two cats already waiting for me in the meeting room. I spoke to Teri. "Good morning. Did the cats bring a toy yellow bird out here?"

"Haven't seen a toy bird of any color."

We never found the remains of the cuckoo bird. The cats, appearing very innocent, watched me as if expecting to be questioned about the disappearance of the little bird. But I said nothing to them about the incident.

Trooper began to growl suddenly, at something in the meeting room. I went to investigate.

He was sitting on the floor, his attention focused on a small table that pressed against a wall.

"What's he growling at?" Teri asked.

"The stuffed squirrel."

"What for? He's seen that squirrel every day for the past year, since you brought it back from Kentucky."

The mounted gray squirrel was a souvenir I found in an old sporting goods store in my hometown of Louisville and brought back with me to Las Vegas for a special purpose, one that had nothing to do with the cats.

I learned over a period of time that some residents of Las Vegas, at least the ones who had lived there the entirety of their lives, had no idea of what a squirrel actually looked like. I thought it might be a fun experiment to have one on display at our office in order to enjoy the comments of our visitors.

I went through quite a bit to implement my experiment. First of all, it was difficult to find a stuffed squirrel in Louisville. People throughout that part of the country, as well as farther north to the Canadian border and south to the Gulf of Mexico, hunt them. Some eat the little gray creatures, but taxidermists get very little profit from them, considering the time involved mounting a squirrel; this held true even for the larger fox squirrel. My find was nicely mounted on a small log for realism.

The mystery of the squirrel's identity to some native-born Las Vegans is based on the fact that there are no such animals in the Vegas valley. They simply haven't seen one. Squirrels are, indeed, found in the nearby Spring Mountain Range, where there is an ample supply of water, natural food they require, and trees to climb and live in; all of these are in short supply in Las Vegas.

Most of our visitors recognized the mounting as a squirrel, and only inquired as to why I had the thing. I explained that it reminded me of my old home, where so many of the gray creatures play about the yards. But the fun came with visitors who had no idea of the animal's identity. One guessed it to be "a large gray rat"; another stated that it had to be a "baby fox."

Of course, Trooper, like most natives, had never seen a live tree squirrel. He paused on the first day I placed the mounting on the table to sniff it and assure himself it was dead. After that, until this day, he gave it no attention. But now the two cats sat staring at the squirrel, as Trooper continued with his growl, which changed in volume from low to high and back to low.

"I think he is trying to teach Brother in the art of growling," I said.

Teri laughed. "Well, he's not doing a very good job of teaching. For the past five minutes all Brother did was meow."

I went to my growling cat, kneeled down, and gave him a hug. He struggled to free himself, and the growl continued. Then the noise stopped, and he peacefully placed his head on my shoulder. I stroked his back and released him.

"Aren't you afraid he'll bite you, Dad? He seemed awfully angry!"

"No," I said, laughing. "He wasn't angry. But, it's wise to know the difference in his mood."

"That's easy for you! I don't think anyone else should try to give him a hug, or even touch him when he's growling!"

"Chi does it now and then. She knows when the growl is play or just a bluff."

While we talked, the two cats disappeared out the door to seek a different adventure. But a few moments later, Brother raced in, leaped atop the table, and bit my squirrel, sinking his teeth into the dry skin and ripping a three-inch section from its side. With the section of skin held in his mouth, he dashed back outside.

Teri and I looked at each other in astonishment.

"What was that all about?" she said with a laugh.

"I have no idea," I answered. "I don't think Trooper put him up to doing that. Something the little cat did on impulse, I guess."

"What are you going to do with your squirrel now? It looks sick with that hunk out of its side!"

"Guess I'll turn it around and face it in the other direction."

She responded with a chuckle.

Then the radio came alive with my wife's voice.

"Please come to the kitchen."

"Who?" I teased.

"You, of course."

I joked with my wife over the fact that her generation of Japanese seldom used familiar, affectionate words such as "honey," "sugar," or "baby," as Americans often do when addressing a special person. Thus, her request would never be "Honey, please come to the kitchen." She found my use of such words cute, but strange.

"Come through the front door when you get here," was the next request.

"Okay. On the way!"

She met me at the entrance.

"I want you to see something," she said, taking me by the hand. She led me to the kitchen.

There, sitting on the back stoop was that ugly cat, the one and only Fat Face.

"What's he doing out there?"

"He was sitting there a little while ago when I first opened the door. He makes a funny grumbling sound and looked so hungry. So I opened a can of food we had after the black girls left. He ate one can and then another. I gave him a bowl of water, too."

"Maybe that's all he wanted before, just food." I said.

"I'm sure. He is so hungry! Maybe he doesn't want to be rōnin. He has no choice. No one to love him."

"What makes you think so? He's just a feral animal."

"He let me pet him when I gave him food," she replied sternly.

"Well, I wonder what Trooper will do if he sees Fat Face out here?"

"He has already seen him! Trooper came up here. He walked up to the stoop. They looked at each other for the longest time, like they were talking . . . only no noise."

"Trooper let him eat?"

"Yes. They didn't fight or even growl."

"Very strange," I replied. "Let's feed him on the stoop, as long as Trooper doesn't object. Don't let him come in the house."

"Maybe Doctor Marg can find him a home like she did for the black cats."

"Going to be difficult placing that fellow. But who knows. Someone may want him."

There must have been something about our ranch that attracted so many different kinds of creatures. I had become convinced of that after the arrival of Fat Face. But he was not to be the last of visiting animals.

It was a bright sunny morning, perhaps a week after the arrival of Fat Face. Chiaki's voice came over the two-way radio with a strange announcement.

"Big bird drinking in fountain! Really big bird with long tail."

Teri and I were at the desk in the office. I shot her a puzzled look.

"Just another bird?" Teri asked.

As a semi-isolated ranch, we have our fair share of winged visitors, including ravens, road runners, and a variety of smaller birds. But never had Chi referred to any of those as "really big bird."

"Where are you, Chi?" I spoke to the radio.

"On the front porch," came the fast reply. "Brought a can of food out for Fat Face. Thought I would feed him in front of Herman's house."

I noted a slight giggle to her voice and moved to the open door for a clear view of the fountain.

"What is it, Dad?" Teri said as she reached my side.

There, indeed, was a really big bird with long beautiful tail feathers enjoying a drink from the fountain. Its blue neck appeared to reflect the sunlight. The bird turned to look at us, then took another drink as he bent his long neck down to the water.

"It's a peacock," I finally answered.

"Where did he come from? They aren't natural to the desert, are they?"

"No, they're not natural to the Mojave Desert, so I have no idea where he came from. The only one I have ever seen was at the Brookfield Zoo in Chicago. I took you kids there years ago."

"Yes. I remember that zoo trip."

"He must belong to someone. Escaped a pen, I guess."

Chiaki's voice came through the radio again. "Is that bird dangerous?"

"No. He won't hurt anyone," I replied.

"Good," came the answer. "I'm going back inside."

We laughed and then began to explore possibilities as to the origin of our visitor. Meanwhile, the bird hopped to the ground and began to strut about the yard dragging the train of tail feathers behind. Teri suddenly grabbed my arm.

"Here comes Trooper," she said with some concern.

Apparently the cat had been watching the bird for some time. Trooper crossed the driveway, lowered himself to a rush and attack position, and began to creep towards the peacock. He did not know what kind of bird confronted him. It made no difference to the cat. Surely the bird appeared to him as a big dinner with lots of feathers.

Bobcats prefer to attack via ambush, initially hiding and waiting, then dashing a short distance to their prey. But this time Trooper changed his strategy. He rushed directly at the peacock. The bird flapped his huge wings and lifted with considerable noise to the lowest branch of a nearby tree. He had avoided Trooper's attack by moments. The cat circled below the bird three times while I held my breath. Trooper, of course, had the capability of quickly climbing the tree to reach the bird but didn't seem interested in doing that.

"It doesn't seem like Trooper really wants to catch that bird," Teri observed with relief.

"He knows that the bird will just fly to another tree. I think that Trooper was only trying to chase the bird away," I answered.

"Trooper waiting until after dark," Herman concluded as he joined us. "He can catch that bird easy after the sun goes down."

"We can't let Trooper kill that beautiful bird, Dad," Teri quickly interjected.

Before I could respond, Chiaki joined us.

"This place is like zoo. That is what I married, a zookeeper," she teased. "Where did you get him?"

"I didn't get him," I snapped. "He just showed up. Came to visit, I guess."

"From where?" she pushed.

"I have no idea. The bird can fly but I don't know how far. We'll ask old Jim. Maybe he knows where the bird belongs."

While our conversation continued, Trooper apparently lost interest in the bird and casually strolled past us and into the office. But I knew my cat well, and I was certain that he had not lost complete interest. He would wait and see how we humans reacted to our newest visitor. The cat would rest while considering his next course of action. If we rejected the bird, tried to chase it away, or indicated any anger towards it, then our action would send a clear signal to

Trooper. He would be clear to take the next action and that would surely be sad for the bird.

Little Brother made an appearance. He wandered out from the front porch where he had been observing the activity and joined Trooper for a nap. But now it was feeding time for Fat Face. I'm not sure where he was during the Trooper-bird confrontation, but he appeared from the back of the property, moving slowly to the front of the guesthouse where Chiaki now waited with a can of cat food. Like most cats, Fat Face instinctively knew when it was time for a meal.

The cat leisurely approached the open can of food. Suddenly I heard a rustle of feathers. Looking at the tree, I saw the bird leap from his branch and glide to earth. He hit the ground running directly towards Fat Face and the can of food. Fat Face saw the bird coming but he wasn't about to be robbed of his dinner. He also raced towards the can, beating the bird by a second or two. Reality set in quickly—the bird was much larger than Fat Face. The cat back away as the bird began to peck at the food.

In a minute it was all over. The peacock strutted to the fountain for a drink. Fat Face approached the can. Empty! The bird had eaten it all.

Chiaki had watched the race from only a few feet away. "Poor Fat Face," she said in a teasing but understanding tone. "Come on. I'll get you another can of food and feed you on the back porch, away from that mean old bird."

The next day she attempted to feed the cat again in front of the guesthouse and, once again, a race between cat and bird began, with the bird winning. It was obvious that she could only feed Fat Face at the back of the house or wait until after dark when the bird would be roosting. We had noticed that as the sun began to disappear each evening the bird flew to the top of a seven-foot wall that separated our front and back yards. There he remained all night, safe, he believed, from all dangers.

Trooper knew how to reach the top of that wall. He had scaled it many times by climbing a large pine tree, which also provided him access to the roof of the guest house, and dropping onto the wall from a branch. The peacock was prepared for intruders at night. Perhaps his only defense was an ear-piercing call to announce the arrival of any intruder. Trooper did not like that call. It surely hurt his sensitive ears so he decided not to threaten the bird, at night, at least for a while.

After a few days of moving cat food around and worrying about the bird's safety, I decided to do some research and see what I could learn about our feathered visitor. I now knew that peacocks could fly, but how far? And what food should he be eating? I instructed Teri to call the Brookfield Zoo, near Chicago, and get the aviary department on the line so I could get some answers. I knew that the zoo not only had a wonderful variety of exotic animals on exhibit but employed a very knowledgeable, friendly staff.

She soon had a zoo representative from the aviary section on the line and I explained our dilemma. "Is it OK for the bird to eat canned cat food?" was my first question.

"Well, Mr. Johnson," she replied with a slight laugh, "Cat food has some ingredients which may, over time, harm your bird." My bird! I wanted to tell her that the peacock wasn't really my bird but held back to keep the conversation flowing.

"Just think of him as a big chicken," she said with authority.

How strange, I thought. "No. That bird is anything but a chicken. He has no fear of a mean tom cat or our pet bobcat, who is just as large as the bird."

She replied with another laugh, "I didn't mean that kind of chicken. I mean to say that he is similar to a farm chicken, the cluck-cluck kind, at least generically he is."

"Oh," I answered shyly. "Then, what should we give him to eat?"

"Peacocks are omnivorous. They will eat most anything— seeds, bugs, flowers, and even small reptiles. But ultimately, they need protein-rich food. No doubt he'll find some of what he needs in your yard. He'll take care of any bug problem you may have. His former owner may have given him cat food so he may have been attracted by the sound of the can opening. I suggest you offer him some quality poultry grain, not cat food."

I thanked the zookeeper and told Teri to toss out some bird seed we held in a barrel in the garage; that could keep the peacock well fed for the time being. Later that day we were visited by Jim Butler, the true eyes and eyes of the neighborhood, who at first stated that he had no knowledge of a peacock ever flying into our neighborhood. Then he added, "I know that they can make a lot of racket with that cry of theirs. I've heard them before when our ship pulled into a harbor in India."

Jim appeared to be in deep thought for a few moments. Then, with a nod of his head, he added, "Maybe the bird came from Wayne Newton's ranch."

"Wayne Newton? The entertainer?" I puzzled.

"Just a thought," Jim admitted. "Newton cares for a bunch of birds and horses at his ranch. At least, that is what I saw on the TV news."

"But," I noted, "Newton's ranch is at least twenty miles from here. I doubt if the bird can fly that far."

Jim agreed and started for the door to leave. There he paused, turned to me, and said, "Come here, you have got to see this! Looks like we have a standoff between bird and bobcat."

Teri and I joined him at the door. There on the driveway, about twenty feet from us, Trooper was in a crouched position, his short tail twitching. He was ready for combat. Another fifteen feet in front of the cat, the big bird stood with all his tail feathers erect. They appeared like a huge fan of brilliant colors, blue and green, with each feather overlapping the next by only an inch. They all sported the famous large eye spots. For some reason, Trooper had confronted the bird and learned a male peacock's first defense. Actually more of a bluff: those tall feathers reaching a height of seven feet, complete with the eyes, were intimidating. It all gave the appearance of a giant, colorful hydra with a hundred eyes, all focused on the cat.

This must have been a shock for Trooper. But he didn't remain shaken for long. With ears flat back against his head, he began to slowly circle the bird, perhaps looking for the best angle of attack. As Trooper moved, the bird also turned and began to shake his feathers, which produced a loud rustling sound. That was enough. Trooper paused and looked over at me as if to ask, *what should I do now?*

"Come over here, Troop," I said in a firm voice, while slapping my hand on my right thigh. This was a way I often called the cat to come to me, and it had occasional positive results. "Come on, Troop. Let's go inside the office."

Teri and Jim stepped aside as the cat entered and leaped upon our desk.

"Standoff is over," said Jim with a laugh. "I'm going home."

I went to my desk and gave Trooper a hug and stroked his back to reward him for obeying my command. A few minutes later, Teri told me that both Little Brother and Fat Face were napping in separate places in the meeting room. Trooper had fallen asleep on my desk. With all the cats slumbering and everything under control in the office, I decided it was time to do a little gardening. I had never been interested in starting a garden of any type, but my love of fresh tomatoes won out over my disinterest. The day before I had purchased a box of twelve little tomato plants and was excited to get them into the ground. I carried the box of plants from a shelf in the garage to the back of the house.

I decided to plant the tomatoes against the house where they would receive good sunlight in the morning, but would be protected from the hot afternoon sun by shade. While digging the little holes in the soft, warm earth, I looked up to see that big bird standing about fifteen feet away. He had cocked his head in order to study me and remained in that position until my project was complete. I started for the house to wash my hands, satisfied that I had completed a perfect planting job. I knew I had a long wait for my favorite vegetable to grow but could, in my imagination, already taste those juicy tomatoes.

Chiaki went out to inspect my work, then I heard her call me. "Where are your plants? Maybe you come out here and see something."

I was at her side. "What is it?" I questioned.

"Look!" She pointed to the peacock, who stood only a few feet away, still looking at us. One of my tomato plants was dangling from his beak. The bird had apparently waited for me to go inside, then attacked my garden, pulling up each little plant and eating them one by one. At first I was angry, but the more I thought about it, the entire event seemed humorous. The Brookfield Zoo expert had noted that peacocks are omnivorous. I now knew that its diet could include tomato plants. A day later we saw the bird making a meal out of bugs he pecked from the front of Chiaki's car. I never tried gardening again.

A few nights after the bird ate my tomato plants, Chi and I returned home from a fast food dinner and witnessed a disturbing scene. It was about an hour after sunset and darkness had conquered the desert. Our car's headlights captured the peacock frantically running in circles about the front yard. I turned off the ignition and noticed Herman standing at his guesthouse door.

"What is that bird doing, Herman?"

"He is in panic," came the answer. "He played around the yard too long and didn't fly up to the wall before the sun went down. He can't see in the dark and knows he is dead meat if he stays on the ground all night. So now he is freaking out."

"That is so sad," Chiaki said. "What can we do to help him?"

I thought for a moment and then came with up with a plan. I instructed Herman to get the big spotlight we kept in the garage and turned to Chiaki. "Get the flashlight from the glove compartment."

I backed the car up and turned the headlights to bright as I drove forward a little. The wall became illuminated completely.

"Herman, Chi!" I shouted. "Point your lights at the top of the wall while I keep the headlight pointed there."

The plan luckily worked. The bird, upon hearing our voices and seeing all the light on the wall, rushed towards it, flapped his wings, and flew to the top.

"Well, he's safe for the night," I said with a sigh of relief.

Chiaki took my hand and squeezed it. "You're such a smart zookeeper," she said with a giggle.

"Starting tomorrow," I responded seriously, "we're going to find a nice home for our big bird. Then I'll put a real effort towards finding one for Fat Face. I think Trooper will be happy to have his ranch to himself again."

I had become worried that the peacock could, indeed, be in danger and that Trooper's tolerance of the bird might be reaching an end, the conclusion of which would not be pleasant for the bird.

"And Little Brother?" Chiaki seemed worried and her question had come with some reluctance.

"Oh, Little Brother is no problem. The two cats are real pals," I assured her.

By noon the next day, Teri was successful in locating the phone number of a bird sanctuary run by the Nevada state government. It was situated on over two thousand acres, only five miles north of town. Two men in a van from the sanctuary arrived that same afternoon with plans to take our big bird away.

"Do you think you can catch him?" I shot the question to the smaller man.

"You bet," the man replied with confidence. "We do this almost every week for folks who want to give us their bird . . . usually a peacock."

"Don't harm him," I replied rather sternly, not yet convinced that the men were professionals at catching birds.

"Don't worry, sir."

The bird stood in the middle of the driveway inspecting us as we talked. The man approached the peacock from the front, attracting his full attention while his partner moved slowly behind the bird. Then he slipped a soft cloth bag over the bird's head, scooped up the bird, and carried him gently to the rear entrance of the van. The action was swift and the peacock neither struggled nor made a sound.

"Don't worry, mister," the first man assured me, "less than an hour and your bird will be running about with new friends, others of his kind. We have eight peacocks and they have lots of room to play. Lots of trees to roost in and all kind of good food. They don't fly away. They have everything they need at the sanctuary. It's like a retirement home for birds. And all under the protection of the state of Nevada. Can't beat that!"

I thanked the men and in another moment, our big bird was gone.

"I hate to see him go," Teri said as I entered the office. "He was so beautiful, but I guess it is for his own good."

"Yeah, he was sure beautiful and very interesting," I noted. "But I did worry about how long Trooper would put up with him. Now we can get busy and find Fat Face a good home."

"Promise, Dad," Teri insisted, "that there won't be a sanctuary for him. Let's find him a home where someone will love him. Despite his ugliness, he is a very sweet cat."

"Yes," I agreed with a laugh. "When I think of Fat Face I'm reminded of something my old boss in Chicago once said . . . you can't judge cats by the quality of their fur."

"He was speaking about people as well, right?"

"Oh, I'm sure he was, but it's true here too."

Not wanting to waste any time, I phoned Doctor Marg and spoke to her directly. She laughed when I described Fat Face, and said she had an idea. She promised to get back to me soon.

I walked to the office, joined by Chi. Teri met us at the door.

"Look at that," she said, pointing towards her desk.

Fat Face lay on the floor, resting peacefully, with Herman standing nearby.

"That is devil cat!" Herman sternly said. "Big, ugly cat! Who does he belong to?"

"I think he belongs to no one," I answered.

"What are you doing out here?" Chi said to the cat. "Trooper going to be mad."

Fat Face sprang to his feet, trotted into the meeting room, hopped onto a chair, and curled up into a ball.

"He's actually pretty well behaved," I said to Chiaki. "See how he responded to your question."

"Poor thing," said Teri. "I petted him when he first came in here. He makes a funny grumbling sound. What do you think that means, Dad?"

"Don't know. Maybe his purring mechanism is broken. But he sure looks happy right now."

"He just needs love and food," Chi interjected.

At that moment, Doctor Marg returned my call, letting me know she already had a home for Fat Face. An elderly lady living in Pahrump, Nevada, was seeking a "big cat companion." Her own cat had passed away a few days before of old age, and she was feeling very lonely. She would drive to the doctor's clinic to claim the pet, providing he had all his shots, and we could deliver him to the clinic tomorrow. We agreed to all this, and I would pay for Fat Face's vaccinations.

Early the next morning, Herman and I approached Fat Face soon after he finished a can of food, and to our relief, the feline let us lift and place him in the car. I was pleased to learn that he, unlike Trooper, appeared to actually enjoy the trip, offering no objection when we carried him into an examination room and introduced him to Doctor Marg.

"I'm surprised Trooper didn't tear this cat apart!" Doctor Marg exclaimed after I related the unusual and unexpected behavior of my buddy midpoint during our visit.

"Maybe Trooper had pity on the cat," I replied. "I was mostly worried about Little Brother."

"I doubt if this old cat would have seriously harmed Brother. When kittens have grown to Brother's size, older cats usually don't kill or seriously harm them."

I thought about Fat Face as we drove home. In a way, he reminded me of Schultz, the tough-guy neighbor from our old house, whose outward appearance of being tough perhaps also covered up a softer side. And maybe that was all Schultz needed, love, even the love of a cat, to change him into a pleasant individual.

A few days later, I received a phone call from Doctor Marg, who gave a very pleasing report. Fat Face had become an indoor cat since living with the lady in Pahrump. He was eating well, gaining weight, and especially enjoyed being rocked to sleep in his owner's lap as she sat in her grandmotherly rocking chair. I smiled with contentment at hearing that news.

Everything in our life seemed peaceful as we settled down that night. Fat Face had a new home, and our cats had been busy chasing one another about the house until, like children, both fell to the ground exhausted. Our new desert scenic tour business was prosperous, and our health, when age was taken into account, was good.

With both cats asleep, I was ready to drift off into dreamland as well.

But just as I was drifting off, the cry of a cat in distress pierced the silence. Immediately the long and haunting yowl of a coyote followed.

Both cats jumped up and went to the edge of the bed. Brother appeared frightened, although I don't think he had seen a coyote. But, that memory was enough. He returned to my side and remained very still.

Trooper held an alert position, sitting with ears forward and nose twitching.

Another yapping and howl, this one farther away, seemed to answer the first call.

"What's going on?" Chi asked, her voice trembling.

"Coyotes! At least two."

"Oh no! I thought I heard a cat screaming."

"You did, but not anymore. I'm afraid to guess what happened out there. The coyotes are coming closer to the house now."

"Don't let our cats go out."

"Don't worry," I assured her. "Brother is right next to me." And looking for the older one, I shouted, "Come here, Trooper!"

The big cat turned his head towards me, but held his position for another few minutes. Finally, to my relief, he lay next to my right leg and fell back asleep. There were no more coyote calls until near dawn. The danger had passed for now, and all was well.

But the next day nevertheless started with excitement. Teri arrived with her three girls and they began at once to play with Little Brother, who enjoyed the attention. He purred loudly and rubbed his head against the children's' legs as a sign of affection. Trooper, on the other hand, had always been cautious when children were near, perhaps because he knew their movements were fast and unpredictable. As my grandchildren, all under the age of ten at the time, chased and played with cuddly Brother, Trooper quietly vanished and retreated to a more peaceful spot somewhere outside to take a nap.

Eventually, Teri and I decided that the noise level from three giggly children had reached an intolerable point, so we encouraged them to go outside to play.

By then, even Brother seemed to have had enough and fell asleep on our desk.

About thirty minutes later, my eldest granddaughter rushed into the office in a panic, tears streaming down her face.

"Grandpa! Grandpa! Something horrible!" she cried.

Teri jumped from her desk. "Where are your sisters?" she screamed.

The child was sobbing uncontrollably, unable to answer.

I rushed out the door. Herman was walking towards me, his arms around the two younger girls.

I released a deep breath. "Are they okay?"

"Of course," replied Herman. "They're upset. But they are okay."

"What has them in a panic, coyotes?"

My first fear was that the children had encountered a coyote, or even worse, been attacked by an animal.

"I watch them play," Herman proudly assured me. "I follow then down near the gulley. They found a dead cat."

"A what? What cat?"

"Don't know. I will show you."

I spent a few minutes with Teri, consoling the children and calming them down with a drink and a snack. Then I joined Herman to investigate the scene. We found the remains of what had once been a beautiful, longhaired calico cat. His belly had been ripped open, but there was no indication that the killer had attempted to eat him.

"Coyote did that," Herman announced sternly, shaking his head.

"Yes. We heard a cat scream last night. I guess this was the one. Then the coyote howling . . ."

"I heard them!" Herman acknowledged.

"Even if I rushed out here, I would have been too late. Get a shovel. We'll bury him here."

"I'll do it," Herman bravely volunteered. "You go back to the girls. Tell them I will bury cat."

"Why did those damn coyotes bring this poor cat here to kill him? Why not in the desert?" My anger had overpowered the sadness for the death of the cat.

"Wolf gave you message, warning. He will come again. That's how he can keep you frightened."

In a way, Herman spoke the truth. The coyote is a member of the wolf family, closely related to the grey wolf.

I was startled by Trooper, who brushed against my leg, then moved to sniff the dead cat.

"Do you know him, Trooper?"

Trooper looked at me a moment, his eyes narrow. I, of course, would never know if he recognized the dead cat. Had it been his friend, a casual acquaintance, or a total stranger? But, nevertheless, I intuitively knew that he felt the killer's presence.

Now the enemy had brought their reign of terror to our property. They killed that cat, not for food, but for pleasure, and perhaps, as Herman suggested, to send a message: they planned to attack us, and soon.

Trooper walked with me back to the office, where I found the children busy with coloring books and crayons at the conference table. As young children are able to do, they were blissfully forgetting the day's encounter.

Herman buried the cat at the spot where it died and placed a small wooden cross that had he assembled from twigs and string on top of the grave.

When I told the children what Herman had done, they rushed out to see the results.

In a few minutes the oldest girl returned, this time a big smile covered her face.

"Grandpa! Come see!" she insisted.

I took her hand as she led me down towards the gulley. There were her two sisters, on their knees, next to the grave. Wild flowers they had recently picked lay across the small mound of earth.

"We are praying for the cat, Grandpa. We don't know his name, but God does, right?"

"Right," I said with a smile.

"Would you like to join us for one prayer, Grandpa?"

I bit my lower lip and replied, "Of course." We kneeled together and prayed for the feline.

CHAPTER 21

The War

"We cannot, without becoming a cat, understand the cat mind."

St. George Jackson Mivart, London

THE COYOTES HAD BEEN OUT there again the previous night, howl-ing, sending a message of terror throughout the community. Once again sounding very close to our home, their cries kept us awake until dawn. The pack had seemed to change tactics and be-gan attacking during daylight hours, as well as after dark. Coyotes are intelligent animals and therefore adapted quickly once they dis-covered that humans were keeping their pets inside at night for safety. No one expects a coyote attack in the daytime. But a few days prior, that had all changed.

The mutilated remains of the cat we had found the day before was without a doubt the handiwork of a coyote, and the bodies of two small dogs discovered by their owners along our country road, less than a mile away, only confirmed a neighborhood-wide hypothesis—the coyotes were no longer killing only for food. They had become thrill-seeking killers, delighting in the attempt to destroy any living creature their size or smaller.

Over the next few days, I spoke with several neighbors, who shared the same anger, to discuss the slaughter of pets in our area. A vigilante-like atmosphere had taken hold of normally nonviolent families who were all now ready to "take up arms" to fight the coyotes. The last testimony I heard came from Jim Butler. "I saw the three coyotes kill Mrs. Stein's cute little white dog, a bichon, I think. Only a puppy," he reported with anger in his voice. "She was walking him on a leash when the coyotes came from different directions. They snatched that pup, leash and all, right from her hands. They carried it across the street and tore it apart as she screamed for help. I got after them with my rake. Too late. They ran off."

Jim paused to catch his breath, then continued. "The next day those animals tried to attack a two-year-old boy playing in his sandbox in their front yard. His mother saw them coming, grabbed a rifle, and killed one. The other two ran off. We hoped they would go back into the desert where they belong, but, no such luck."

"So, now there are only two?"

"That's right," Jim replied, wiping at his brow with a blue bandana. "A large one, tan with some black color in his coat, and one about half his size, tan and small but fast. I'll shoot 'em both if I ever get the chance!"

After Jim's disturbing report I finally accepted what everyone else already understood: that those two coyotes must be destroyed before they killed again. They were now dangerous to both animals and children.

The police were of little help. Jim called them once, via the 911 emergency number, but by the time they responded to the call, the coyotes had vanished. We were too far out of town and police cruisers seldom patrolled our area. Federal wildlife authorities gave standard advice: "keep children and pets inside." That was of little comfort.

It was as if war had sliced into our community, a war with terrorizing beasts who killed for no good reason, and as with any war, almost everyone had suffered the loss of something they loved. The brutes had, as per Jim's last report, killed and eaten all but a handful of Ruth Parker's guineas.

I had often encountered coyotes during desert scenic tours. Because we as humans are visitors in their wilderness, the idea of harming one never entered my mind. But now the situation had altered dramatically. The coyotes had invaded our territory and were killing at random.

The thought of Trooper being killed by a coyote both angered and sickened me. The cat and I had become so very close since I rescued him as a kitten more than a dozen years before. We had played together in the house and yard. He had taught me how to stalk and use shadows at night for concealment. We had napped together and often ate at the same time. At night, the cat curled up next to me and I wrapped my arm around him as we fell asleep together, listening to his purr.

Usually, at some point during the night, he would leave to explore, returning at dawn to resume sleeping. At 6:30 a.m. he would wake me so I could begin my daily activities. He would follow me about the grounds and often took a nap on my desk in the office as I waded through mountains of company paperwork.

Since coming to us, Little Brother followed Trooper everywhere and copied his routine. Unlike his companion, Brother was an ordinary tabby, more interested in simply playing than hunting or learning much of anything.

These cats were not just pets—they were members of our family. And I would protect them as such.

I had succeeded in domesticating Trooper, helping him grow from a wild bobcat kitten to a lovable, ordinary cat. True, he was a rather big one, but his friendly nature was like that of a domestic cat. At times it seemed we were alike in certain ways, the cat and I. We knew each other's feelings with a glance. So it is with very close friends. *Had I made a mistake? Should I have let him retain his wild nature? What would he do if confronted by a coyote? Had he retained the wild instincts necessary for his survival?*

All those thoughts haunted me as I prepared a cup of coffee the morning after my conversation with Jim. I shuffled to the kitchen door and opened it. Fresh desert air swept into the room through the screen and the opening cut near the bottom, which the cats used as their favorite entry.

While sipping my coffee, I gazed out the kitchen window to enjoy a view of the rear of our property. Trooper and Brother were not there. I assumed they might be visiting Teri in the office. That visit was part of the cats' morning routine preceding their snack and noontime nap. Alternatively, they could be on some adventure in the wooded gulley which separated our property from the desert wilderness.

Suddenly my heart leaped out of my chest. Near the far corner of the property a large coyote had begun a slow approach to the kitchen door. I stared in disbelief. A coyote in my backyard in daylight, bravely trotting towards the house! Jim Butler had described him perfectly: it was a very large coyote with some black color in a tan coat. *Where was his hunting companion? The other coyote must be on the property, but where? Why had they divided forces? Were they that confident of success?*

The coyote lowered his body and slowed his pace to a crawl. Perhaps he planned an ambush near the kitchen door, knowing the cats would soon return for lunch.

I set the coffee cup down and rushed to the bedroom to retrieve my .45 automatic. I pulled the receiver and let it fly forward, locking one cartridge in the firing chamber. I returned to the kitchen, lay flat on the tile floor, and began a slow crawl towards the door. My movements were not visible from outside as the screen mesh of the door reflected sun rays. I inched on, staying at an angle from the cat hole. If the coyote came close to the door, I could, with careful aim, shoot through the opening.

The crouching coyote had closed the distance to only twenty feet from the concrete stoop. He paused. Had he heard my breathing? I tried to hold my breath as I aimed directly at him through the hole. I would have only a second to fire. It had to be a fatal shot.

I didn't want to wound the animal. He had brought so much sadness to my neighbors; I'm sure each would take the shot if given the opportunity.

Now he was only about twelve feet away. He raised up with nose twitching as he tested the breeze. His chest was in my sights. His eyes widened. He must have detected my scent. I squeezed the trigger. The report of the pistol was deafening, but my aim was good.

The bullet struck the coyote in the middle of chest and the shock of the impact knocked him backward. His body twisted once and he fell dead.

I stood up and stretched to calm my nerves. I was not accustomed to killing anything. I gulped down the remaining coffee and lifted the two-way radio from its charger. Where were my cats? Where was the other coyote? I started to push the talk button of the radio to see if Teri could already be at her desk, when her voice came on, startling me.

"Dad!" she called from the radio. "What's going on up there at the house? Did I hear a shot?"

"Yes," I answered. "I shot one of the coyotes. He's dead. There is another one, but I don't know where he is. Have you seen Trooper or Brother this morning?"

"Haven't seen Trooper. Herman just walked in. He says he saw Trooper down in the gully about thirty minutes ago. I saw Brother from my window. He was playing with a bug at the base of the big pine tree. Stand by! I'll take another look."

While waiting for her response, I moved through the front doorway and headed for the office.

From her window Teri had a panoramic view of our narrow side yard directly outside the office. It sloped southward, then dropped several feet into the gully. I was near the end of the office building when her voice came through the radio again.

"Dad! My gosh! A small coyote just entered the side yard from the east!"

"What's he doing?"

"He's a few feet out from the building, moving slowly. He's almost directly under my window now. Oh, no! I think he's going after Little Brother!"

"Where is Brother?"

"He's still at the pine tree. Brother turned. He sees the coyote! Why doesn't he escape up the tree? The coyote knows he's been spotted. He's slowing down to a crawl."

"I'm almost there," I spoke between breaths. "I'm at the end of the office, coming up behind the coyote . . . about thirty yards east. I'll try for a shot when I get closer. Bang on the window and try to distract it."

"I already did that. He's programmed for Brother. I don't think anything will distract him! Hurry, Dad! Brother doesn't stand a chance. He's too small!"

"I'm turning off the radio," I said, placing it on the ground.

I could see the coyote clearly and there was Brother, nonchalant as always, using his front paws to play with something. Then the golden kitten began to roll about in the dust, flopping over and snapping a quick look at the coyote. He seemed to be taunting the enemy, daring him to come closer. I wondered if he knew something both the coyote and I did not.

That silly Brother. Why doesn't he scamper up the tree before death reaches him? I wanted to shout at the kitten and tell him to jump, but he was too young to understand. At his age the world held wonderful games to play each day and a never-ending display of things to explore. He could no more understand that the world contains evil than he could comprehend my commands.

My gun hand shook, even when I tried to steady it with a grip from my left. If I fired, I might miss and hit Brother, and unless I hit a vital area on the coyote, he would still charge at the kitten, covering those last few paces in seconds.

Then, from the corner of my eye, I thought I saw a movement to my left, in the gulley, but it had moved so very slowly. *Perhaps it was my imagination? There! It had moved again!*

Now I knew that Trooper was in the gulley stalking the coyote, quietly matching its pace, safely out of sight. Little Brother was not so silly after all. His rolling game teased the coyote, holding its attention as Trooper moved closer. But what would the big cat do if he came up from the gulley? Would I witness the slaughter of two friends I loved dearly?

The cat knew I was nearby. Though we exchanged no glances, still, he felt that I was there, and somehow I understood his thoughts. My pulse quickened and my breathing felt labored. *Was it stress and anxiety?* Maybe my system suffered from the traumatic experience a few minutes ago when I killed an animal, or was overloaded with my fear of losing the cats.

But then those feelings disappeared quickly, and were replaced by a strange sense of invincibility. As I recall now, my legs were steady, not shaking. Yet a part of me seemed to be lifting . . . as if floating away. I was drifting directly to Trooper. I became aware of every smell, and every sound had intensified. The sage, creosote, and even the sandy earth where I stood emitted different aromas, all stronger than I ever than any I had ever known. I became tense, yet somehow felt strength in every muscle.

My breathing returned to normal, and a wonderful, contented sensation trickled through my body. My eyes saw color, brilliant and out of focus at first, then sight returning with unbelievable sharpness. I knew now that I was with Trooper. We were moving together. We were the same being. Our feelings, as the result of years of closeness, had brought us together at this critical moment. Efforts to turn or back up were useless. I felt propelled on and on, drifting in a helpless state. And then confidence replaced that helpless feeling.

I was not really moving, yet I felt each paw step the cat placed, quietly, one in front of the other, pause, then one in front of the other, oh so slowly . . . slowly.

We were moving up from the gulley and lowered ourselves to the ground. The grass brushing my stomach as we inched towards the enemy. We knew we must attack. It would not be a hit and run warning. Now it would be a final fight. We would aim to kill, even though we might die. So it is in the wild.

The fur on our back and neck bristled, amplifying our appearance. Our eyes were wide open, fixed intently on the coyote. Our minds registered every move he made. Our long whiskers were forward; our large, pointed ears lay back in a protected position.

There was an urge to rush the coyote, but we knew we must resist that temptation . . . for a moment longer. Closer, a little closer.

How the coyote hated that kitten. The desire to tear Brother apart for being such a tease must have been overwhelming. That held his attention, which had locked in on the kitten.

Our breathing slowed, each breath deep and calculated, and our mouth became wet, lubricating our teeth for combat. Attack now!

Suddenly I felt the thrill of speed as we dashed forward, charging to close those last few feet. The wind cooled my face as it rushed past. I felt us spring into the air and the thrill of a brief flight. I felt us smash into his back and the salty taste of blood. Trooper had sunk his fangs into the coyote's neck at the base of the skull.

I released a deep breath and tilted backward. I had been released from that strange dream world and became a human spectator once more. My mind, in any state, dream or awake, could not completely comprehend the ferocious fight before me. Two wild animals, almost equal in weight and size, were locked in a mortal combat.

With his superior stalking, the cat had remained silent, and he gave no warning during that swift attack. But once they locked together their growls were horrifying, the sounds echoing through the desert. At that point of impact, Little Brother finally decided it was time to dart up the pine tree and rest on a large branch.

Trooper's claws sank deep into the coyote's back, securing his grasp as the enemy began to jerk left and right in an effort to free himself of the cat. Then the coyote ran in tight circles, stumbling twice before falling on his side. The cat's bite stunned the coyote. The bite was crippling, but not lethal.

As the two warriors hit the ground, the coyote attempted to roll and trap the cat beneath him. But that move provided the exact opportunity the cat needed. As the coyote started to roll, the cat released his grip and sank his fangs into the side of his enemy's neck, just below the jaw. The cat's head jerked from side to side as fangs ripped the throat. Blood gushed from the bite, then slowed to a trickle.

The coyote's legs twitched and his chest heaved for a moment. Then he was still, utterly defeated. It was over, but Trooper's jaws remained locked on the enemy's throat. He held that death grip for a minute or two longer, finally releasing his defeated foe and crawling backward a few feet. Trooper lay on his belly, front legs stretched out towards the coyote, rear haunches raised, ready to leap. He watched and waited. Then he stood and crept slowly towards the coyote. With whiskers held back against his cheeks, he leaned forward, placing his nose against that of the enemy. His whiskers moved to the front. I worried that the coyote might be faking death and spring back into action.

The cat was not concerned. He smelled death and his nose confirmed the victory. While humans, in checking for life, feel for a pulse at the neck or wrist, or listen for a heartbeat, the cat uses his keen senses and checks for breathing.

Trooper backed away from the dead coyote with his eyes wide and ears erect once more. He turned and slowly walked in the direction of the kitchen door, pausing only to rub his cheek against my leg. I was so proud of him. I thought nothing of the blood stain left on my pants leg by his gesture of friendship.

"Good boy, Trooper," was all I managed to say.

Little Brother leaped from the tree and, ignoring the dead coyote, ran to catch up with his hero. With his golden tail held straight up, he joined Trooper's side and they both began a trot to the house.

Teri was next to me. "My gosh, Dad," she exclaimed. "I watched it all from the office window. It was so surreal! I didn't know a bobcat could take down a coyote, but I saw it!"

"If the coyote got the first bite," I said, "it might have had a different ending. But the cat was too fast."

"I wonder if Trooper remembers that coyotes killed his family and almost killed him when he was a kitten? He got his revenge."

"A cat never kills for revenge, only for survival or to protect what he loves. Trooper used another one of his nine lives today."

"Dad," she began with a concerned tone, "I was thinking. What will Trooper do now? I mean, he returned to the wild for a few minutes. Will he remain in a wild state, or will he be our loveable cat again?"

"I really don't know," I confessed. "We can only wait and see which life he decides to live."

CHAPTER 22

Introducing Brother to the Desert

Neko kye gari. (A cat's love is unconditional.)

Japanese expression

WE HAD A PEACEFUL NIGHT for the first time in over a year, with no coyote howls to haunt our dreams. Neighbors began to let their dogs and cats out after dark, without a worry about them disappearing in the jaws of coyotes. Children would be permitted to play in sandboxes and on backyard swing sets without worry.

The first night following the battle, Trooper and Brother remained in my bed through the duration of the night, only venturing out come dawn. It seemed that the big cat was exhausted and Brother simply chose to stay with his hero.

But Chi might have realized the true reason: Trooper wanted to show his devotion to us after his brief return to the wild during the battle. Nevertheless, we'll never be sure why he changed his sleeping routine.

Soon after, I tricked our fuzzy warrior and got him into his travel crate with little difficulty, as we went to visit Doctor Marg. I wanted her to examine him for wounds, though I didn't really expect her to find any. And deep down, I felt the need to relate the battle story to someone outside the family.

Teri was given the assignment of cat-sitting Brother and keeping him entertained in the office until we returned. The entire office was a wonderful playground for Brother, so I didn't think she would have any problems.

Doctor Marg listened quietly to my saga of cat versus coyote as she searched Trooper's body for injuries. As usual, he remained still, enjoying her touch.

"There is nothing wrong with your friend." she announced happily. "Physically, he's fine."

"What about mentally?"

She laughed. "You're the best judge of that. You two have been pals for a long time. If the fight bothers him, you'll know it. But I doubt if it ever will. He did what was natural for him—kill an enemy, protect his friend. He may worry about your acceptance of his actions, but he doesn't worry about social influences at all . . . not like we do after an accident or, say, a fight. Now, what did you start to tell me when you came in here? What did you call it? 'A strange mental experience'?"

"Well," I hesitated. "I haven't told anyone but my wife. I'm sorry. I didn't expect to have you become a psychiatrist."

The doctor chuckled, and then I noticed her large shoulders were sloped forward and her short cropped dark hair was streaked with gray. The three of us had aged. I had not realized that fact before. She continued to lightly massage Trooper's muscles.

"You're getting too old to be picking fights," she suddenly said.

"You talking to me or the cat?" I said.

She turned and stared into my eyes.

"Both of you," she said, smiling slightly. "Go on with your report! Trooper survived the fight. Did you?"

I looked down to the floor, contemplating just how to answer. Should I be honest, or avoid the question by pretending she was not really expecting a reply? "I actually felt . . . believed I had become a cat . . . for a few moments!" I finally said.

"Go on . . ." she encouraged as she turned her attention to Trooper.

"It never happened before, that feeling. I felt his movement, his thoughts . . ."

"His thoughts? Interesting."

"Yes, interesting. But now that I think about it, it is frightening." I paused, waiting for a response. None came, so I continued.

"What I mean about his thoughts . . . I knew what he planned to do. How he planned his stalking, his attack. I could feel it, even though I couldn't see him clearly."

"Why not?"

"He . . . we, it seemed, were creeping up slowly from a gulley, moving between bushes. Then, I felt us leaping towards the coyote."

"Mr. Johnson," she interrupted, "you and this cat have been close for what, thirteen years? That's a very long time. It's not unusual for two creatures who feel strongly for one another to believe, in some way, they are the same."

"Yes. I can agree with that."

"So, why not you and your cat? People often become totally, emotionally involved with a pet. In your mind, during the fight, you were giving the cat encouragement, helping him with the attack."

"That is what I've considered."

She switched tactics. "Do you watch football on TV?"

"Very seldom," I responded. "Not much time to sit that long, no matter how exciting it is."

"Well, you know many men do."

"Yes. Of course."

"My husband, for example, gets very involved during the Super Bowl. He, his brother, and a friend all jump from their chairs, knock things around, yelling and screaming at players thousands of miles away. My husband even cradles a football in his arms during the game. I think that he feels he is running with the real ball carrier, racing for a touchdown!"

She laughed and waited for my response.

It was dawning on me now. "I think I see the similarity."

"You have the answer, Mr. Johnson. Nothing should concern you about your experience. My husband loves football. When he watches it, he's involved emotionally, and almost physically. You love this cat. What's the difference?"

I thought about her explanation as scenes from Trooper's fight with the coyote flashed through my mind

"Thanks, doctor," I responded, though still not fully convinced my experience was identical to her husband's.

Trooper was unusually quiet during the drive back to the ranch. I wondered if, in his thoughts, he was reliving his battle as I had briefly done during the conversation with Doctor Marg. But I had learned something from the cat through my experience with him over the years. Of course, it was difficult to know with any certainty but I think he had a way of placing many events, especially troubling ones, from his mind and would continue on with new things he believed important. Life goes on, so to speak. Did he forget past events? I don't think so. He simply avoided places, things, and people that made him uncomfortable, the same we humans do when we are thinking logically.

As for me, I too had to clear my mind and move on to current projects.

Once I opened the crate upon returning home, Trooper leaped out and bounded towards the office. That was his first priority of the day. After assuring Chiaki he had suffered no damage from the fight, I walked out to get a report from our cat-sitter. It wasn't what I expected. "Dad, that little cat is more trouble than a three-year-old in a china shop!" Then Teri added, pointing, "But he still is silly-cute. Look at all those things on the floor next to the book shelf."

She continued with her report, almost out of breath.

"He jumped up on the shelf and knocked everything off. Then I scolded him and he came to the desk begging for attention. He's quite a paradox! One minute full of mischief, the next begging for affection."

"Well," I responded, "he's sleeping in a chair in the meeting room now."

"Good! He wore himself out getting into trouble."

Indeed, the little cat was sleeping peacefully, joined by Trooper, who apparently was still stressed from his trip to the doctor.

My attempts to discipline Brother had, in the past, also been unsuccessful. If I scolded him with a stern *No!* or a sharp *Brother!*, his feelings seemed crushed, and he pleaded to be cuddled and stroked. He would remain a very sensitive cat throughout the years which resulted in us giving him more freedom than necessary.

Perhaps part of our reluctance to discipline him was because he often responded to the situation by being a clown. He had some strange desire to entertain through acrobatics and an unending series of fast movements that consisted of leaping high onto something and tumbling off in very un-catlike crashes.

We simply concluded that Brother craved attention, and we usually succeeded in meeting his needs.

Trooper, on the other hand, was far less tolerant of Brother's demands. Perhaps, because of his age, he was a little cranky or just didn't want to be bothered, so the big cat often smacked his mischievous friend—of course, with no claws extended. Brother would then rush to one of us with large sad eyes for consoling.

"That is a very funny cat!" Herman announced while standing in the office doorway one afternoon.

I joined him to see what had the man amused. In the front yard, under the shade of one of our tall cottonwood trees, Brother was busy digging a hole in the soft, sandy soil.

Trooper sat a few feet away, appearing to supervise the project. Brother continued to dig to a depth of his chest. Only his head was visible.

"What's he doing, Herman?"

"He's digging toilet! That's the way he always prepares his toilet. I've seen him do that before."

"Why so deep?" I said, puzzled. "Cats usually don't dig that deep a hole."

Herman's shoulders hunched. As clueless as I, he walked towards the guesthouse.

Once again, Brother had caused a comical incident, though this one was probably intended to have been intended to be a little more private. As ridiculous as his deep toilet appeared, the project remained important to him for several weeks. Apparently, the refilling of the hole required extra energy even a young cat was unwilling to exert. He finally decided a much shallower hole would suffice.

During Brother's hole-digging Trooper sat back several yards away and simply observed the activity. I think that Trooper found Brother's potty "training" amusing. A bobcat, in the wild, may bury his waste, or leave it exposed if he is marking his territory. We seldom saw Trooper in such a situation but when we did, the hole he dug was shallow. Over the next several months I noticed that Brother's potty hole became shallower and eventually not deep at all. We never learned why the original hole was so deep, but the excavation seemed important to the little cat.

"We have a serial killer, Dad," Teri announced one morning with obvious disgust. "Trooper has a small, down-like feather on his whiskers!"

"One feather doesn't make my cat a serial killer."

"Yeah, but he had a similar feather on his whiskers yesterday!"

"Maybe it was the same feather!"

"Come on, Dad . . ."

"I think he needs a good lawyer," I joked. "You can't convict a cat on circumstantial evidence."

Trooper had begun a sincere effort to teach Brother the art of hunting and stalking, beginning with a short run and a leaping attack.

Brother attended those classes, conducted "in the field," but I believe in his heart he was a pacifist. He never indicated even the slightest interest in killing anything. He was a loyal friend, however, and did accompany Trooper.

I watched early one morning, shortly after sunrise, as Trooper moved slowly from the gulley on the desert side of our ranch and began to stalk something. Brother followed closely behind, mimicking his friend's movements with little enthusiasm.

Then I saw their prey: two desert tortoises. Each was about twelve inches in length. Their high-domed, dark brown shells appeared dusty in the morning sunlight. Apparently they had just emerged from their burrows where they would, no doubt, return once the heat of the day made life uncomfortable. In fact, more than 90 percent of the life of a desert tortoise is spent underground. They live in burrows from early October until sometime in April, depending on the warmth of the sun. If the young, when hatched, can survive predator attacks by hawks, ravens, coyotes, and bobcats, these plant-eating creatures can live over fifty years, some reach the age of eighty in the Mojave Desert. They obtain the water they require from the cacti and other plants they eat and store it under their shell to survive during hibernation periods.

The tortoise is listed as a "threatened species" under the Endangered Species Act (1973), and in Las Vegas, they are also protected by the Bureau of Land Management.

One of the stalked tortoises flipped the other over onto its back. I don't know if they were fighting or playing, but I worried that the reptile would remain helpless, unable to return to a normal position. I learned later that they can often right themselves, but if not, of course, they die a slow death.

There, helpless upon his back, his legs waving frantically, the poor reptile struggled as Trooper closed in.

I prepared to rush through the gulley and rescue the tortoise when I noticed that the other tortoise had returned to his victim and flipped him back into an upright position. Was this an act of compassion? Had the stronger tortoise planned to teach the other a lesson?

Meanwhile, I continued my race to prevent Trooper from attacking, but I was too late. He rushed at one, but stopped inches from the reptile. Then he reached out with his large paw and gently touched the shell. By now, the tortoise had safely retracted his head and legs.

Trooper looked over his shoulder and sat down, waiting for Brother to join him. The cats sniffed the tortoise and then casually returned to the gulley.

It seems that the big cat had no intention of actually killing the reptile. He was conducting a training exercise in the art of stalking and rush attack. In this advanced training, Brother must learn how to attack a fast-moving target, one that could possibly escape.

Trooper had encountered a tortoise before. He knew they moved slowly, at least much more slowly than a jackrabbit, and would hide in their shell without fighting back. For the cat, the reptile was a great training tool. No harm would come to Brother, though the exercise must have been traumatic for the tortoise.

The next day a true test awaited Brother, one which would require extreme stealth and speed. While watching this exercise, I realized that Trooper knew they were attempting the impossible: to capture an elusive bird.

It was a good education for his young friend, with no plans to turn the prey into dinner. The impossible target selected was a raven.

The southwest common raven is a highly intelligent, large black bird standing up to two feet tall, often weighing over four pounds. The bird has played a key part in the life of man for thousands of years, especially in ancient mythology, religion (the raven is mentioned in both the Bible and the Koran), music, and literature.

Because of the raven's glossy black plumage, deep croaking call, and diet of carrion, it was considered a bird of ill omen by some ancient cultures, while others have thought it to be a powerful and helpful symbol. In Greek mythology, for example, the raven was a sign of good luck.

Ravens had a very special place in Norse legend. Their chief god, Odin, owned two ravens which he named Huginn, or "thought" and Muninn, or "memory" (or mind). According to the myth, recorded over 1,200 years ago, the two ravens served as Odin's eyes and ears and were given the ability to speak, at least to Odin. Each morning the birds flew about the world, returning in the evening to report to Odin what they saw and heard on their travels. (A curious aside: Odin worried that someday Muninn would become lost and never return.) In Viking lore, King Ragnar Lodbrok honored the raven with its image on his banner, carried on both his ship and into battle.

In the Mojave Desert today, we have no buzzards or vultures to feed on carrion and, with the exception of the loss of coyotes and jackrabbits, very little roadkill. This doesn't bother the raven. It will eat just about anything—insects, berries, or small animals—to survive. The raven often mimics the sounds in his environment, including human speech. They mate for life, the male demonstrating considerable devotion to his female. On the ground they run, hop, and move about in a strut-like walk, but in the sky they are beautiful flyers in spite of their large size, using wind currents to conserve energy as they bank and glide in graceful pairs. They are known to be aggressive and will attack predators if one nears their young, and can be very cunning, often dropping stones on their enemy in an attempt to injure or kill. But most of the time, unless threatened, they are curious, playful birds, always working in pairs.

Trooper had attempted, unsuccessfully, to catch ravens over the years. With all his stealth ability, the ravens still detected his advance and escaped to the sky. While one bird fed and strutted about the ground, its mate remained high in a tree, telephone pole, or something similar, keeping a watchful eye for danger. On a signal, its mate took to the sky. Occasionally both birds would land in the same area, and Trooper often took advantage, with no luck, of those rare occurrences.

So when Herman reported that Trooper and Brother had been "hiding" in the culvert pipe under the road for over an hour, I decided to investigate.

I sat under the large pine tree, the same one where Brother had taunted the coyote two years prior, and waited, my eyes scanning the desert opposite the gulley.

Then I saw a large raven, his glossy black feathers reflecting in the sunlight, devouring something between sage bushes. His mate perched upon a telephone pole, standing guard, ready to sound an alarm.

Trooper emerged from the pipe slowly, followed by Brother, who always appeared clumsy no matter how hard he tried to duplicate the big cat's movements.

I realized that Brother was about to receive the ultimate stalking lesson. Trooper had selected the impossible task of sneaking up on a raven, but strictly for practice and educational purposes, I'm sure. He wanted his young friend to learn the bird's tactics. But attempting to catch the most intelligent bird in our sky was a challenge.

The cats moved slowly up from the gulley. Trooper was the first to reach the top, and as he crouched and prepared a dash for the bird, the mate on the pole sounded the alarm with a deep croak.

Trooper rushed the target and missed by several inches as the bird launched safely.

Easier kills, such as quail, doves, and sparrows, awaited. I doubt if Brother learned anything that day, or cared. He wanted to accompany the big cat, but as he reached the age of three, he would still rather play than hunt.

Trooper and Little Brother sat, side by side, statue-like, eyes fixed on the oven. The wonderful aroma of roasting turkey filled every room in the house and must have been overpowering for the cats, whose sense of smell is so much stronger than our own.

Chiaki and I had developed a technique of stepping around the cats as we went about preparing a variety of dishes for the Thanksgiving meal. This was a difficult chore, as we expected eight guests, employees, and special friends for the big dinner.

Chiaki remained composed and efficient, as always, in the kitchen, even though I am sure she was frustrated, stepping over the "oven-watching cats."

My job was simple. I set the big table in the dining room, got a strong fire underway in the living room fireplace, and ensured the small, portable bar had all the necessary favorites, including red and white wine, bourbon, vodka, scotch, and, of course, a big container of chopped ice.

I completed all that, then answered her call to come to the kitchen and remove the golden-brown turkey from the oven.

The cats watched her with anticipation as she sliced off a thin section of white meat and chopped it into small pieces on a plastic plate. She then led the cats out the door to the back porch stoop where they could finally enjoy their portion of the Thanksgiving meal.

I opened the front door to welcome our guests, who all arrived at about the same time. I was greeted by a crisp, cool breeze. A gray, overcast sky provided a foggy view of the Spring Mountain Range in the west. Their high peaks were already snowcapped.

The guests had no difficulty finding the bar. Then they gathered about the fireplace in casual conversation.

I lit the candles on the dining table and assisted Chiaki, hauling the bowls of food she had so carefully prepared.

Soon, the long awaited announcement: "Let's eat!" A second call was not necessary. My friends behaved as if they had not seen food for days.

I said a short prayer and then turned everybody loose to help themselves to the food that was already being passed around: mashed potatoes, sweet potatoes, green beans, biscuits, stuffing, turkey, gravy, and cranberries.

Conversations began to fade as everyone was busy loading their plates and preparing to feast. From my position at the table, I could enjoy a panoramic view of our side yard through the large, tinted picture window that was directly above the cat door. It was the one through which Trooper had forced in the unconscious owl the year before.

The voices of my guests began to fade as my thoughts drifted and my eyes fixed on the beautiful pine trees outside. Then, Trooper appeared, entering the scene from the right. He carried what appeared to be a dead desert quail in his mouth, his big ears erect, short tail pointing straight out. He sat down and placed the quail in front of his paws. Nothing unusual with my bobcat so far. Trooper often captured desert creatures. Some he ate, and some he released unharmed.

I glanced back to the dinner table. Chiaki was receiving deserved compliments about the meal.

My eyes returned to the window. Little Brother had entered from the left and taken a seated position directly in front of Trooper. The two were separated by twelve or fifteen inches and one dead bird. A meeting of felines was underway. Now it really had my attention. It appeared as if they were about to partake in some sort of ritual.

As I have noted, the behavior of cats has always fascinated me. I was constantly attempting to understand their needs, motives, and just how they communicated important (to the cats) information. What were the important matters? I am still convinced that felines communicate by some sort of mental telepathy.

Nonsense, say those who have never loved and lived with a cat. It is all controlled by simple animal instinct. So let's review the rest of this episode.

To my knowledge, Little Brother had never killed a bird nor any animal. He followed Trooper on hunts, observing the kill, but, always the pacifist, never participating. Nor did he eat any "wild game," preferring instead his canned and dry cat food or anything he might snatch from the kitchen table.

Although it might appear that Trooper was now offering the quail as a shared dinner, I knew that wasn't the case. And Trooper knew that his little friend wouldn't eat that bird.

They sat there, staring at one another over the dead quail for at least four minutes.

What could the two cats be discussing? What was that meeting all about? To me, the scene was much more interesting than the human conversation at the table.

Then, to my surprise, Little Brother suddenly picked up the quail in his mouth, presenting a very funny sight. The bird was one-third the size of the cat, who struggled to find the correct balance to carry it. Brother trotted out of the picture, and in a moment, Trooper had also disappeared.

With that brief show over, I turned once more to the dinner table. Everyone was much too busy with the feast to notice that my attention had drifted away. No one saw the golden, fuzzy cat enter at the cat door, a dead quail locked tightly by his jaws.

I thought, at first, it best to remain silent and not alarm the guests, thus also giving Brother time to take his bird somewhere in the house.

Brother paused for a moment, as if considering his next move. He reached the far end of the table, and with a graceful leap, landed in full sight of all, next to the gravy bowl.

He then, head erect with pride, strolled towards me. Guests stopped eating and seemed to place their forks down in unison.

"Oh, no!" someone exclaimed.

"What has he got?" another asked.

"A bird! It's a dead bird!"

"Oh, *ugh*!"

Ignoring the less-than-complimentary comments, Little Brother sat down in front of me and carefully placed his bird inches from my plate. He looked up at me, his big eyes pleading for praise.

No one but Brother heard me whisper, "You are such a good kitty. Thank you very much!"

One couple had already left the table and were moving towards the bar. They would miss the rest of the show.

Brother looked about the table, then placed both front paws on his bird. With rapid jerks of his head, he began to rip the small feathers from the bird's breast. Downy feathers began to float above the table, landing softly on the mashed potatoes, cranberries, and beans.

Things were happening fast, like frames from an old silent movie. The remaining guests were up from the table and joining the first couple at the bar.

I heard the voice of Herman call out: "Brother is preparing your meal, Johnson!" I'm not certain that was the case. I think he was performing a ceremony he had witnessed Trooper do so many times.

In those few seconds, and while chaos had control, I managed to pick up Little Brother and two slices of turkey and head to the back door in the kitchen.

Trooper sat on the back porch stoop as if expecting us. I sat Brother down and tore the turkey apart, ensuring each piece landed on the plastic plate Chiaki had placed there only an hour before.

"Did you put Little Brother up to this?" I snapped at Trooper.

He didn't answer. Both cats were busy cleaning their dinner plate.

I returned to an empty dining room. But Chiaki was still at the table, waiting for me. I expected to see tears rolling down her cheeks, but she wasn't crying. She sat, stone-faced, eyes expressing no emotion. Then I feared she might be in shock, but she wasn't.

"Would you like something to eat now?" she asked quietly.

"I'm sorry," I mumbled. "You worked so hard to make this dinner."

I picked a feather from my plate.

"You have turkey," she replied, ignoring my apology. "Mashed potatoes?"

"Yes, thank you," I answered.

"With feathers or without?"

I looked up. Her face was now etched with a slight smile. Then the smile began to beam with understanding.

I laughed. "No feathers, thank you!"

My alcohol-consuming friends appeared to be recovering from the shock of a most unusual Thanksgiving meal, which was never completed.

I apologized to each person separately. It was as if I had a child who had misbehaved. It is hard to apologize for that.

I was informed that while I was removing Brother from the table, Herman had disposed of the quail. Of course, feathers remained for days.

One thought continued to haunt me. Had Little Brother only given the bird as a gift, as cats sometimes do with their catch? Or had Trooper planned a complex scam, using simple Little Brother to carry out the action? Was it a gift with bad timing, or was there much more to it?

I find all that difficult to comprehend, but. . .we had a lot of "leftovers" that weekend.

CHAPTER 23

The Touching of Heads

"If having a soul means being able to feel love and loyalty and gratitude, then animals are better off than a lot of humans."

James Herriot

"MR JOHNSON, YOU HAVE AN intruder in your home. The signal is coming from the hallway, near the master bedroom door."

The calm voice of the security system operator on my cell interrupted an otherwise peaceful dinner my wife and I had, to that point, been enjoying at a nearby Italian restaurant. I set my fork down and thought a moment before replying.

"But if someone is in the hall, he or she would have had to come through a window or door. Do you notice a breach at one of those points?"

"No, sir. None."

"Then how did they get in?"

"I don't know, sir. Maybe through the roof . . . or a hole in the wall. Our equipment only picked up movement in the hall."

"Could my cat have set off the alarm?"

"Not unless he is five feet tall. The intruder had to be at least five foot to activate the motion detector."

"My cat is big, but not that big."

"We have sent one of our armed response cars to your home and notified the police. No one will enter the property until you arrive."

"Good. We're on the way."

I placed money to pay the bill and tip on the table.

"What's going on?" my wife asked worriedly as I escorted her to the door.

"I'll explain in the car."

As we drove from the parking lot, I phoned Herman and instructed him to remain inside until the security company or the police arrived. I didn't want him wandering around outside the house and have the police mistake him for the intruder.

When we arrived at the house, the police officer, a large flashlight in hand, advised that he, the security representative, and Herman had already checked the outside of the house and found no sign of forced entry. I unlocked the front door, deactivated the alarm at the keypad, and stepped back to the let the officer lead the way.

An hour's search of the house uncovered nothing unusual. Even the cats were nowhere to be found. I assumed they were playing outside and would avoid the excitement created by strangers. Chi later told me she noticed that both Trooper and Brother were sitting calmly in the shadows of the guest house, watching.

Days went by and the odd incident of an "intruder" was all but forgotten. The alarm people brushed it off as a possible "malfunction or temporary interruption in the electrical system," whatever that was supposed to mean.

But things are rarely that simple, and a week later it happened again. This time we were driving home from another restaurant when a call came from the security company. Otherwise, the scenario was identical. A search of our home revealed nothing unusual, nor did it produce a five-foot-tall intruder. The mystery bothered us for a few days more until an answer came while we were watching television one night in the bedroom.

By now, Brother had become a full-grown cat, but was still very playful and mischievous. Trooper, on the other hand, was beginning to show his age. His naps were frequent and longer, and his weight had dropped from twenty-eight pounds to about twenty-three. But he still had bursts of energy, racing and chasing Brother about the house and yard, but with a nap to follow that vigorous exercise. Those racing games were exactly what activated the alarm system.

While I had initially suspected that the cats were to blame, I wasn't sure how they did it. Brother never had the ability to jump straight up to a height of five feet. Trooper, at a younger age, easily obtained that altitude, but in later years limited his jumps to mostly straight out, not up. In his old age he still climbed trees with remarkable speed, often pouncing down upon an imaginary prey.

We discovered the answer to the motion detector mystery by accident.

Outside our bedroom door was a small space where a metal, spiral staircase led to a second-level storage room. Both staircase and that room were seldom used . . . by humans.

The cats, however, had added more fun to their chasing games by running up the spiral stairs and springing off to land on the floor, six feet below, thus causing the motion detector to activate an alarm. So, our "intruder" was not a five-foot person, but rather jumping cats.

The alarm company disconnected the detector in the hall, and our evenings were never interrupted by their calls again.

Walking out to the office a few days later, I heard Brother meowing frantically. Trooper sat in the driveway in front of the guesthouse door, staring intently at something on the roof.

Looking up, I saw Brother racing along the roof's low wall, meowing frantically as if he was being chased. I knew, instantly, his problem. He had followed Trooper up the pine tree to the roof, and now either could not remember how to come down, or lacked the nerve to try. I watched for a few minutes. The poor gold cat was panicking. There was only one solution. Trooper must go up and show him the way down. But apparently, to that point, the big cat had no interest in doing so.

As I studied the situation, I became convinced that Trooper, in his own way, was trying to teach Brother the special technique required for roof climbing and, more important, returning safely. The student obviously had not learned.

I worried that Brother might jump to the driveway, a distance that was too far, even for a strong cat.

I made Trooper follow me to the base of the tree, lifted him up, and held him until he grasped the trunk. He understood what I wanted him to do and quickly climbed to the large limb that reached over the roof. That limb served as a sturdy bridge to cross from tree to roof, but apparently it did take nerve to jump back onto it for a return trip.

I stood there, trying to see just how Trooper would show the little cat the best way to escape the hot roof, but their activity was hidden by the wall. Then, I saw the limb move a little as Trooper appeared on it near the trunk. He started down the tree, head first, to lower limbs, turning halfway down, then continued tail first a few more feet, turned again and leaped to the ground, an art he had mastered many years ago.

The big limb moved again, and there was the brave Little Brother, moving cautiously, step by step, so unsure, but he succeeded in returning to earth.

After letting out a huge sigh of relief, I soon settled down to do some paperwork at my desk, and was in a pleasant conversation with Teri, when my wife's voice blasted through on the two-way radio.

"Come quick!" she yelled. "Meat-eating cat!"

I frowned and answered, "Chi, what did you say?"

"Meat-eating cat!"

I looked at Teri, who had a broad smile. "What's she talking about, Dad?"

"Don't know. Trooper is asleep on a meeting room chair. Guess I had better get up there."

"Where's Brother?" Teri asked.

"I thought he was out here. He came down from the roof some time ago."

I jogged to the house and found Chi standing in the kitchen, her hands on her hips.

"What is this meat-eating cat you're talking about?" I asked with a laugh.

"It's not funny," she snapped. "I was preparing two small filets for us for dinner . . ."

"I see one," I said, looking at the plate in front of her. "Where's the other?"

"Yours . . . is over there," she replied with a slight laugh. "With your meat-eating cat!"

She pointed to the corner of the living room where Brother crouched and chewed on the raw hunk of filet. He sat up, the beef between his front paws, and stared at me with his big eyes, pleading for mercy.

"I had the meat on the plate," she explained, "and turned to look for the garlic salt in the cabinet. Like a flash, that cat jumped up here and ran off with your dinner."

"Why my dinner? Could we share your little steak?" I tried to hold back my laugh. Somehow, I didn't feel angry. This was rather funny.

Suddenly Brother rushed past us, the steak dangling from his mouth, and dashed through the cat entrance in the kitchen screen door.

"There goes your dinner," she stated coldly. "You had better have a talk with that cat."

I followed Brother as he raced towards the office. By the time I reached the meeting room, Trooper was awake and enjoying the remaining piece of meat the little cat presented to him.

Peeking from out behind Trooper, Brother's eyes seemed to plead for mercy and forgiveness. Maybe he believed we might say nothing to Trooper and that the big cat would protect him.

"What's going on in there?" Teri asked.

"Oh, nothing, just my cats eating my dinner!"

"What?"

"Never mind, Teri. Could you please order me a pizza? Deliver here about six."

"Sure, Dad."

Our neighbor, Jim, once said, "Your bobcat has probably test eaten every creature in this desert, his size or smaller."

Perhaps that was true, but I noticed that Trooper showed less interest in hunting as he aged, and seemed to be very content with his favorite dry and canned food. He had, in a way, reverted to a young cat again, from a dietary standpoint, anyway.

That was fine with Brother. I don't think he ever once ate anything that could move of its own volition. Even when Trooper brought a "kill" to him, he ignored it, preferring to munch on generic store-bought cat food.

When it came to stalking prey, of course, Trooper's skills were superior to Brother's, but his goal, with one exception, was restricted to wild animals. That exception was helicopters. He hated those air craft for years. Maybe he thought they were giant birds, coming to avenge all the smaller ones he killed during his life, or maybe the chopping sound of the blades bothered him. As a young cat, he hid under any available protection, but as he grew older, he went into a crouch position, ready to attack the thing if it came close enough.

Perhaps the best example of his intentions came one night while I watched a war movie on our large-screen television. Trooper napped peacefully nearby until he heard the sound of a helicopter on the TV. As the helicopter appeared to come closer on the screen, the cat crouched and began to inch his way to the set. His short tail twitched and he swiveled his hips like a golfer preparing to try a difficult putt.

The helicopter became louder as it flew in our direction. Trooper rose slightly, ready to spring forward. I jumped and tackled him at the same moment as he leaped for the attack. With my arms wrapped around him, we rolled across the floor from the impact of our crash. The second we recovered, the show cut to commercial, and his enemy, the horrible helicopter, was gone. The cat sat up and looked at me as if I were the crazy one, but he pushed his head to my arm in a show of affection. I lowered myself so our two heads could touch, and his eyes widened in acceptance of my gesture.

Differing from Trooper, Brother enjoyed stalking any moving, mechanical thing. Chi and I had invested in a toy firetruck, powered by battery, which was about two-and-a-half inches long. Brother stalked and chased the little truck, chewing on it and tossing it as if it were a mouse.

Unlike most cats, he had no fear of vacuum cleaners and would attack ours as Chi attempted to clean the carpet. His war with that machine became such a hindrance that she often had to postpone the cleaning until Brother had found something outside for amusement.

His greatest fascination was with a small electric train I assembled to entertain my grandchildren when they came to visit. But the train set had a short life.

Like a feline Godzilla, he first attacked the cars, tossed them into the air, and then crushed the tiny engine. The tracks were saved for last. By the time I crossed the room to stop the destruction, only a few pieces remained connected.

Yet Brother's actions, as naughty as they may have been, were comical. His big eyes, appearing always so pleading and innocent, made it difficult to reprimand him. In fact, often before I could say a serious word of criticism, he would come to us, using his head "butting" as part of a negotiation for mercy.

This touching of the head is a wonderful way of identifying you as a friend, sort of a handshake-hug combination. It also leaves their scent behind and can be a method of saying, *You are mine*. Cats use the touching of heads for greeting each other, things, and even other animals. And it isn't restricted to domestic cats. Trooper used the affectionate greeting from the time he was a kitten.

Perhaps the extreme example of this head touching came when the cats discovered a new, very large, strange-looking animal in our neighborhood.

The cats were sitting atop the low stone wall that separated our front property from the road. Their attention had been fixed for some time on something beyond a white rail fence on the opposite side. I joined them to learn what was so interesting. And it was soon apparent: I saw a snorting monster staring back at them, a beautiful chestnut mustang.

I doubt if Trooper had seen a mustang before, so this creature in our area was a new attraction. Even though all the ranches around us were called "horse" property, no one actually owned one, until now.

The famous free-roaming horses of the American West were first introduced to the New World when Cortés entered what is now Mexico, in the early 1500s. The mustangs today are mostly descendants of those Spanish horses, and are technically feral, rather than wild, as their ancestors were domesticated. The actual word "mustang" comes from the Spanish meaning an "animal that strays." But the average American thinks of those horses as wild and free.

As the Spanish explorers journeyed north through the central and southwest regions of North America, they brought their horses with them. Some explorers traveled the Spanish Trail from Southern California, around the Grand Canyon, and into what is now New Mexico. Over many years some horses escaped and survived as strays in the wilderness. Soon, in some areas, the Native Americans found a good use for horses.

In the mid-1800s, American pioneers pushing West traveled with their horses, which had been introduced on the east coast by English, French, Dutch, and German immigrants.

As Americans arrived in the West, some of their animals wandered away and joined the free Spanish horses.

Both the Spanish and American pioneers also brought along donkeys (or burros) and some of those also managed to break free and still roam the Southwest.

The primary government authority for the management and protection of mustangs and donkeys is the U.S. Department of the Interior, Bureau of Land Management (BLM). This organization determined in 2002 that the severe drought gripping the Southwest had, of course, placed the mustangs and donkeys in danger. Most horses and some donkeys were relocated farther north, where they can find the natural food and water needed for their survival.

A few donkeys, with their ability to survive on less water than horses, and possessed of a greater tolerance of natural plants to eat, remain on government-controlled land near Las Vegas, roaming free around the beautiful Red Rock Canyon National Conservation Area.

The BLM has an adoption program through which one may purchase a mustang (or donkey) for about $150, providing the buyer meets certain qualifications, including the ability to provide enough acreage for the animal to enjoy. Most of those adopted animals have become devoted pets and are wonderful for recreational riding.

Our neighbor across the road, to the northwest, owned fifteen acres that had sat vacant for several years prior. Recently he had enclosed it with white rail fencing and taken advantage of the BLM's adoption program.

The chestnut mustang pranced about the property, becoming somewhat domestic, or at least tame, faster than I expected. I confess, I know nothing about taming wild horses.

Before the introduction of the horse to our neighborhood, Trooper, no doubt was the largest animal on four legs. Now, a giant lived across the country road.

I held my breath for a moment as Trooper crossed the road and moved slowly along the rail fence, first one direction, and then back. I think he had determined, through hours of observation from our wall, that the large animal was indeed trapped on the other side of the fence and could not break out. Assured of that fact, it was time for an animal introduction.

That was what worried me. Horses have a very keen sense of danger, especially from predators.

Bobcats, in some parts of the country, have been known to kill deer. They are not foolish enough to attack a horse. But mountain lions do kill horses, and to the mustang, cats may smell the same, regardless of size.

Brother remained at a safe distance, perched upon our wall. Trooper sat very close to the bottom rail of the fence. All of us waited for the horse to react to the cat's presence.

The horse might panic and race about his corral, or worse, break down the rails and escape.

But he did none of that. Instead, he whinnied and walked slowly to the fence. Trooper rose, stretching on his hind legs, until the top of his head reached almost the second rail from the top.

The horse stretched his neck and reached his massive head until the two touched noses, then Trooper's head.

I stood for moments in disbelief, unable to move. Brother raced across the road and at Trooper's side, stood with his paws on a rail and tried to reach the horse's nose. He was too small for the touch and dropped to his feet.

I was both deeply moved and thrilled. Two animals, both from the wild, had greeted each other in peace. This odd friendship would continue as the animals visited one another from time to time.

But I also had an uneasy feeling as I watched Trooper cross the road and return to our yard. He appeared to be moving much more slowly than usual, with legs somewhat stiff, and his big ears, which were always so alert, held slightly to the side.

Trooper and I had been together longer than most people are rewarded with the love of a pet. He was truly at an old age for any cat, especially one who had survived so many life-threating situations, including some I am sure occurred but which I had no real knowledge of. I knew I must prepare myself emotionally for that day when he must leave us. The thought frightened me. I wanted to hide it, bury it away somehow, as I had no way of knowing how to deal with the feelings when the loss came.

CHAPTER 24

Gone

"Don't cry because it's over. Smile because it happened."

Dr. Seuss

"GRANDPA, DO DOGS AND CATS go to heaven?"

My granddaughter's voice sounded very serious and I had to think before giving an answer. It was obvious she had concerns. What is it about children that motivates them to ask sensitive questions when one is busy on unrelated projects? Why not an easy question to answer?

I leaned back in my desk chair.

"Do you think I know the answer to such a serious question?" I replied.

"Of course you do, Grandpa. Mom says you know everything because you've lived a long time."

"Oh," I answered, attempting to hide my smile.

"Well . . . ?"

"Well, yes. I'm sure they do."

"Why? Why are you sure?"

I tried to remember what I had read on the subject of animals and heaven.

"It all has to do with what you believe," I said. "Do you believe that Heaven is a happy place?"

"Yes," she answered firmly.

"What gave you that belief?"

"The Bible. It says Heaven is a place of peace and happiness."

"Okay. I'll tell you what a wise man once said: if you have a pet and you and the pet are happy together, then God knows it. So, when you go to Heaven, your pet will be with you, and you both will be happy, because that is what Heaven is about.

The little girl looked at me with a long gaze, then started to walk away. Had I put her mind at ease? But, as it is with any child, my answer prompted more questions.

She turned to me.

"What about snakes?"

"Snakes?"

"Yes. Robbie, my friend, he has a pet snake. He calls it Eli. Robbie loves Eli."

I had to answer quickly.

"Then, if Robbie loves his snake, they'll be together in Heaven."

The child smiled and added, "Eli never bit anybody. Not yet, anyway."

"Good."

And so my day began with challenging subjects. It was still early. I returned to the papers on my desk, only to be interrupted by Herman.

"Big killing in the garage," he announced, passing by the office door on the way to the coffee pot in the meeting room.

"Who got killed?" I asked.

No answer.

"What's he talking about?" I said to Teri.

"Not sure," she answered, "but I guess it's about the massacre trap set up by Trooper in the garage."

"What massacre?" I laughed.

"You know that twenty-five-gallon barrel where you keep bird seed you bought for the guineas and all the other birds?"

"Yes. I had Herman place a piece of plywood over it to prevent the birds from getting into the barrel for unscheduled feedings."

"Trooper knocks that cover off so the birds can get into the barrel and eat."

"Considerate of my cat."

"That's not his goal, Dad. He uses it as a trap!"

The garage, situated between the office building and Herman's guesthouse, always had a musty odor from oil and other chemicals needed by Herman for his maintenance duties about the ranch. A cornucopia of power equipment, mowers, saws, and tools lined the walls, always in neat arrangement.

Along one wall a wide shelf, about four feet above the floor, remained empty. It ran the entire length of the unit. For easy access the garage door was always open.

Under that empty shelf we had placed a small barrel filled with bird seed, its opening covered with a quarter-inch-thick piece of plywood. We discovered that Trooper could easily push that lid off, permitting birds to fly in and enjoy the seeds. The big cat waited in ambush upon the shelf above, until the barrel filled with birds. Then he pounced down and the "massacre" began.

Trooper wasn't hungry, and this killing presented no interesting challenge or "thrill of the hunt" for him. Brother was with him, waiting on the shelf, but jumped to the floor rather than the barrel and calmly walked away.

What became Trooper's last attempt to teach Brother the art of killing, a very easy kill at that, met once more with failure. The gold cat simply had no interest in killing or eating anything from the wild.

Indeed, this was Trooper's last effort. His ability to jump up onto a platform, a shelf, or desk had diminished substantially. To reach me in bed, he resorted to sinking his claws into the blankets to pull himself up.

I requested Herman to construct a six-foot ramp, covered with carpet, which sloped at an angle so the big cat could easily walk up to me.

Naturally, Brother assumed the ramp was for his pleasure, and ran up and down it a few times before Trooper could give it a try.

The ramp solved the one problem, but did not address the cause, a deterioration of the body due to old age. I had to force myself to be realistic: Trooper was almost nineteen years old, old age for any cat.

I stood on the front porch one morning and watched as he walked slowly towards the office. He paused, sat down, and then returned to the house. He didn't want company that day, and apparently lost his curiosity, unconcerned about who was in the office or what the day's activities might include. Nor was there any effort to patrol his territory any longer.

That day we lay together on the living room floor as we had done many years before. Brother came and settled down at my other side. Trooper offered no objections and we three fell asleep.

We knew we must get the old boy to the hospital, but I dreaded the thought. I placed his hated travel crate on the kitchen floor a few days later. Its top gate was open. Chi and I sat at the kitchen table discussing how we might get him into it without a struggle. Then an amazing but sad thing occurred. Trooper walked into the kitchen, looked at the open crate, and hopped into it.

Chi looked at me for a comment. In all these years we had never been able to get him into that crate without his serious protest.

"I guess he's telling us something," she said. "Do you want me to go with you?" Then she began to cry.

"No. No, it is best you stay here. Keep an eye on Brother. I don't want him to try to follow us."

I gently pushed Trooper down and closed the gate. He remained silent during the trip.

I felt very uncomfortable as we entered the reception area. It had been remodeled since Doctor Marg retired, and I didn't recognize anyone on duty.

"Yes, Mr. Johnson. We received a call. Bring Trooper and follow me to the examination room. Doctor will be with you in a moment," said the young nurse.

"How did you know my cat's name?" I asked.

"Oh, we've never met, but Trooper is a legend around here. The nurse who trained us talked about Trooper all the time."

The tall young doctor entered, introduced himself, and spoke to me with a few professional words. But I didn't remember any of it, and forgot his name when he left the room, carrying the crate with Trooper sleeping inside.

I did remember him saying, "Would you like to wait? This may take a while," or something along those lines. My mind was a mess of jumbled thoughts as I struggled to control my emotions. For a time, everything seemed like a blur, and his words came through as an echo.

"I'll wait," I said.

I waited, sitting alone on the metal bench in the examination room. An hour passed, perhaps two. I had no concept of time.

Finally the young doctor returned.

"I'm afraid I have bad news, Mr. Johnson."

"Yes?"

"We thought Trooper's problem was kidney stones and a urinary tract infection. But that's not all. While he has those conditions . . . he also has bladder cancer and a small tumor."

"Not good," I managed to reply.

"No, sir. It is not good. I would not suggest surgery. Even if successful . . . we remove the stones and tumor, we can't be certain how far the cancer has spread. After surgery, we can't say how long he will live, and the pain he will suffer is something we cannot control."

The doctor paused, studying my reaction. Then he added, "I don't think you want the suffering to continue."

"Of course I don't." I stumbled over my next words. "This is the end?"

"I'm sorry. Would you like to stay with him as he goes to sleep?"

"Yes, please. I can't leave him alone."

Trooper appeared to be asleep on the table in the operating room. But as I came near, his tail twitched slightly. A nurse offered me a chair and I sat at the table, my arm pressed against him. I began to whisper in his ear, "I'm here. I'm here." His eyes opened, then closed. I could hear a mild purr.

I don't think he felt the injection, but I did. A pain rumbled through my entire body, and then, nothing; no pain. *Is that it*, I thought. *Is it all over? Does it always end so quickly?* I stood, eyes flooding, and returned to the metal bench in the exam room.

At least Trooper knew I was with him. He didn't die alone under some bush in the desert. I was thankful for that.

A nurse entered and offered me a cup of cold water, which I accepted gratefully. She said there were papers I must sign before I go, but I could stay as long as I felt necessary. Then, as the girl departed, the figure of a large lady with gray hair entered. I blinked my wet eyes, and to my surprise, recognized Doctor Marg in front of me.

"I didn't expect you."

"It is only a coincidence I am here today," she replied. "I'm so very sorry for your loss, Mr. Johnson. Actually, in a way, our loss."

She came to me and gave me a hug.

"Since my retirement, I stop by once a week to see how the new owners are doing. One of the girls told me you were here. I did look at the test results and X-rays. They were correct. There was nothing medical science could do for Trooper."

"Your opinion always mattered to me, doctor," I mumbled.

"You made the right decision. I've watched so many pets leave us during my career. The loss is always devastating to the owner. This one hurts me. You two, your relationship was so unique. I don't think your situation could ever be duplicated. I wouldn't recommend anyone to try to accomplish . . ." She paused, then continued. "You two had a wonderful adventure. Someone else may not be successful."

"Thank you for all you have done for us over the years. I've been wanting to say that."

"We must remember," she continued after taking in a deep breath, "everything we have is only loaned to us for a while. Be happy for all the fun you two had."

We hugged a farewell. While signing papers at the reception desk they told me the bill would be mailed to my home. I appreciated that small consideration. A nurse attempted to hand me Trooper's travel crate. I requested they dispose of it. I didn't want to see it again.

I sat in the car for several minutes to be sure my hands were no longer shaking. My legs seemed steady, so with blurry eyes I began the drive home.

I found it difficult to believe that so many years had passed since I made that first drive to inform my wife I had adopted a bobcat kitten. Now I had the obligation to deliver to her a different message. This one would be much more difficult.

Chiaki was waiting for me, sitting at the kitchen table. When she noticed I did not have the travel crate, she assumed Trooper had remained at the hospital for treatment. I had to find the strength to tell her the truth.

"Chi," I began while taking her hand. "He won't be coming home. They couldn't save him. He's gone. He didn't suffer at all. He just went to sleep."

She looked at me, shaking her head.

"He had a long life, and we had lots of fun together. Let's try to think about it that way."

She broke free from my grasp, covered her face with her hands, and ran towards the bedroom. I went to the kitchen sink and with a wet paper towel wiped my face. I sighed and sat down at the table. My mind was blank for a time, then a funny feeling came over me. I felt that someone was watching. I looked at the window and back door. From where I sat I could see most of the living room area. No one was there.

The eerie feeling persisted for a minute or two, then I felt comfortable, relaxed as one does in the presence of a good friend.

Suddenly I heard what at first I thought to be a strange sound. No. It wasn't strange at all. It was a *yap*, like a sharp bark. I remembered that sound from long ago. Then I heard the bark again and I blinked my eyes.

It was the same little bark Trooper had used to get my attention, to call me when he was a kitten. The same bark-like sound his mother and all wild cats use to call their young. But why would I think about that now? Of all the things I remembered about Trooper, why would that thought haunt me when I was so vulnerable?

Then I was startled by a voice, calling.

"Johnson!"

I thought I heard a voice, clearly calling my name; it was not a shout or a whisper, only a muffled sound like one might hear in a dream. Then you awake and discover that no one is near. But you are convinced you heard it.

I sniffled and looked about the kitchen again. Empty.

"Chi! Did you call me?" I shouted.

A long moment of silence, then an answer came from the bedroom.

"No! I didn't."

The sadness and stress from my loss had pulled me deep into a pit. At that moment I felt I might never crawl out. I didn't have the strength or will. Was I enjoying the feeling, the wading in my misery down there where breathing becomes difficult?

I knew the solution. I must pull myself from under the shroud of self-pity.

The answer to the pain of loss had always been my ability to drift into the comfort of a fantasy world where there would be pleasant thoughts and sweet memories of happy times with Trooper. In that play world we could once again run and tumble together. I needed so desperately to lose myself in memories, to go back to the time I carried that wounded little cat with the big feet out from the wild and into my world.

Stop it! Get busy with something, I told myself. Save those memories for another time. But how long would the healing take, days or months or years?

Suddenly I realized that while I was lost in my thoughts, Brother had joined me at the table. He sat at the edge, his large eyes fixed on mine, his head tilted slightly to one side, as if he might be listening to something. But there was no sound at that moment.

Poor Little Brother. We had neglected him so much the past few weeks while our attention focused on Trooper and his deteriorating physical condition. We had always held Trooper in higher regard. Like the oldest son, he was special, and he had been with us for many years.

We were kind to Brother, but Trooper received the most attention.

Soon Brother would also feel the loss. How could I explain to a simple cat that his hero was gone forever? Could he already know, and not understand?

"Johnson!"

There was the voice again! Then I realized, with a strange sensation, no one had called my name. I was feeling it. The voice rippled through me, but with no sound.

Had the stress, the sadness, been too much? Could I be hallucinating?

I didn't notice, but Brother had moved closer and sat inches away, those eyes still staring intently at my face. Then he lay down slowly, placing his head on my outstretched arm, his eyes fixed on me.

I once read that cats know the feelings of humans. Could Brother sense my sadness?

I often understood what Trooper was thinking. We would look at one another and I could feel what he wanted to tell me. Our odd but wonderful communication continued until near the end.

I had never given Brother an equal chance to reach me with his thoughts. I had unintentionally shut him out because of other priorities.

"Johnson! Touch him!"

The words were not clear, but still I felt them. I reached and touched Brother's back, lightly stroking his soft fur. He began to purr.

And then I understood. The voice came again, comforting me.

"Johnson, I'm here! Don't be sad. You'll learn. He's really a very fun kitty to know!"

And he still is.

Postscript

ALL THE PEOPLE IN THIS story are real, but some names were changed to protect their privacy.

Shortly after we lost Trooper our life took a new direction. The days of our profitable gift shop were long gone, and bookings for the desert tour business began to slip. This was in part the result of competitors with larger advertising budgets moving into town.

Soon it became impossible for us to cover the high cost of operating the ranch. Perhaps its existence had only been necessary for Trooper to enjoy freedom. Life works that way sometimes.

Teri relocated to the Phoenix area where she would be closer to her twin brother and younger sister.

Herman fell in love with one of our Japanese tour guides, and together they moved to another part of town.

And our surrounding desert began to disappear as the city continued its phenomenal growth.

Jim Butler, our eyes and ears of the neighborhood, sold his property and relocated to a senior retirement community. His "old Navy buddy" joined him there.

We sold our ranch and moved into a town home where Brother became an "inside cat." He appeared to have no objection to his new lifestyle, but I believe he was lonely, and that worried me.

We enclosed the back porch with rabbit-wire fencing, and placed two carpet-covered cat trees with the ramp Herman constructed for Trooper leaning against one of them. This provided Brother with good exercise opportunities.

One day, orphan two kittens made our small backyard their home. They soon discovered they could slip through the four-by-three-inch openings of the rabbit wire and enjoy Brother's dry food.

This feasting continued for a few days until the kittens became so fat they could no longer fit through the wire. Fortunately, they were trapped inside Brother's exercise area.

Chiaki named the smaller kitten BB, and the other, with a peculiar black spot on her nose, Dot Com.

Brother now has two playmates who admire him greatly. We continued our desert tours, on a limited scale, knowing Brother was no longer lonely.

Sometimes the three fuzzy creatures will, as cats do, sit and simply stare at one another for a long time. I wonder if Brother is telling them about places he has been, where they could never go; of the many adventures shared with his big friend; and of how he and Trooper once ruled the desert, or how the two of them outsmarted a dangerous coyote.

Brother had become a very macho cat, though still mischievous and lovable, so I suspect that in his version of those adventures, he was the leader.

We humans, however, know the true story of the cat who came in from the wild.

Acknowledgments

I HAVE LEARNED THAT THOSE who met Trooper never forgot the encounter.

A view of an elusive bobcat crossing your yard or a chance sighting along a trail in some wilderness is a thrilling experience. But entering my office and seeing one peacefully sleeping on my desk was unforgettable.

Though many years have passed since our adventures on the ranch, once in a while I still meet someone who will say to me, "I remember that big, beautiful cat of yours. Is he still roaming the desert?" (or something to that effect).

"Yes. In a way, he's still out there," I always answer.

My wife, Chiaki, became the self-appointed family photographer the first day I brought Trooper home from the pet hospital. Searching through his photo album, I discovered that our collection, as it usually is with our children, was mostly limited to his younger days. We have many photos of him as a fuzzy kitten, or as a chubby young adult. But there are few that were taken after we moved to the ranch and he became busy, enjoying his freedom.

Having the camera handy at just the right moment was impossible. Except at night, or napping in my office, he seldom remained in one place very long. In those days, cell phones did not contain cameras, so getting a photo of the cat in a tree, or in the flower garden, was a matter of luck. Look away for a second and he was gone.

I wish to thank a few special people.

First, my literary agent and friend, Agnes Birnbaum, of Bleecker Street Associates, Inc., New York City. She has unmatched perseverance, with her marketing and editorial skills, and has guided me successfully for over fifteen years.

I write the old way, with pen and paper, and needed someone with the ability to read my scratched-over notes and place them in an acceptable form, electronically. I was fortunate to meet Ms. Marcia Baum, an extraordinarily talented and pleasant lady, who accomplished what seemed to be the impossible. Her efficiency in typing and computer science produced the needed results.

My special thanks to the wonderful people at Skyhorse Publishing, especially editor Veronica Alvarado. I appreciate Ronnie's faith in my story, her sharp eye, and her suggestions. Her professional editorial work was extremely creative and, as a bonus, she is a great pleasure to work with.

Lastly, thanks to my wonderful wife, Chieko (best known by her stage name, Chiaki Keiko). You cared for Trooper from his playful days as a kitten, sat up some nights worrying about him when he was on one of his territorial patrols, and helped nurse his injuries when he returned after a battle. I am forever grateful for your love, understanding, and encouragement, especially as I prepared this biography of our friend from the wild.